PERGAMON INSTITUTE OF ENGLISH (OXFORD)

Language Courses

ANALYZING ENGLISH
SECOND EDITION

EDINBURGH
MORAY HOUSE COLLEGE
SCOTTISH CENTRE FOR EDUCATION OVERSEAS.

Forthcoming in this series

F. AARTS and J. AARTS
English Syntactic Structures
An introduction to units and structures
in contemporary written English

IVAN POLDAUF
English Word Stress

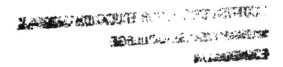

ANALYZING ENGLISH

An introduction to descriptive linguistics

HOWARD JACKSON
City of Birmingham Polytechnic

SECOND EDITION

SCOTTISH CENTRE FOR EDUCATION OVERSEAS
MORAY HOUSE COLLEGE
EDINBURGH

PERGAMON PRESS
Oxford · New York · Toronto · Sydney · Paris · Frankfurt

Shirin
B·ED·TESOL 4·

U.K.	Pergamon Press Ltd., Headington Hill Hall, Oxford OX3 0BW, England
U.S.A.	Pergamon Press Inc., Maxwell House, Fairview Park, Elmsford, New York 10523, U.S.A.
CANADA	Pergamon Press Canada Ltd., Suite 104, 150 Consumers Road, Willowdale, Ontario M2J 1P9, Canada
AUSTRALIA	Pergamon Press (Aust.) Pty. Ltd., P.O. Box 544, Potts Point, N.S.W. 2011; Australia
FRANCE	Pergamon Press SARL, 24 rue des Ecoles, 75240 Paris, Cedex 05, France
FEDERAL REPUBLIC OF GERMANY	Pergamon Press GmbH, Hammerweg 6, D-6242 Kronberg-Taunus, Federal Republic of Germany

Copyright © 1982 Pergamon Press Ltd

All rights reserved. No part of this publication may be reproduced, stored in a retrieval system or transmitted in any form or by any means: electronic, electrostatic, magnetic tape, mechanical, photocopying, recording or otherwise, without permission in writing from the publishers

First edition 1980
Reprinted 1982
Second edition 1982
Reprinted 1985

Library of Congress Cataloging in Publication Data
Jackson, Howard.
Analyzing English.
(Language courses)
Includes index.
1. English language–Grammar–1950 I. Title. II Series.
PE1106.J28 1982   420   81–23534   AACR2

British Library Cataloguing in Publication Data
Jackson, Howard
Analyzing English: an introduction to descriptive linguistics.–2nd ed.–(Language courses)
1. English language
I. Title. II. Series
420   PE1106
ISBN 0–08–028667–4

Printed in Great Britain by A. Wheaton & Co. Ltd., Exeter

for Hilary

Contents

Acknowledgements

This book came into being over a number of years in the course of teaching the analysis of the modern English language to students on the English degree at Birmingham Polytechnic. Like many students of English coming to study for a degree which includes a fair proportion of linguistic work, after the purely literature courses they have pursued at school they find the ways of thinking and the analytical approach required for this work at first often new and strange. I am grateful to all those students who bore with my attempts to find the most satisfactory way of introducing the modern linguistic study of English. I would also like to thank Vaughan James of the Pergamon Institute of English for his help and advice in the preparation of the manuscript for publication. And I owe a debt, as in many other things, to my wife.

HJ

Introduction

Many people associate the term 'linguistics' with the philosophy of language (Wittgenstein and the like), with learning foreign languages, or with abstract mathematical symbolism supposedly charting the language that we speak and write. Now linguistics does have something to do with all these three activities, and the third of them in particular occupies the attention and energies of many scholars working in the field of linguistics. Perhaps the most well-known, but by no means only, scholar falling into this category is Noam Chomsky, who initiated the 'transformational generative' school of linguistics.

Such scholars are often referred to as 'theoretical' linguists. Their aim is to construct a unified model or theory to 'explain' the nature of individual languages and of human language in general. Like all theoretical sciences, theoretical linguistics aims to make as explicit as possible its axioms and procedures, so that its hypotheses and theories can be adequately tested. The explicitness required demands a measure of formalism, and for this theoretical linguistics looks, like other sciences, to mathematics and symbolic logic. This makes many linguistics books daunting to the uninitiated and difficult for the layman to gain access to. Much modern linguistics over the past 25 years has been of this kind, often concentrating on individual problems of description at a quite abstract level.

However, not all linguistics is like that. More important, in the opinion of this author, and complementary to the kind of approach outlined in the previous paragraph is a branch of linguistics referred to as 'descriptive' linguistics. This approach starts with a language as it is spoken and written, with the data of actually occurring utterances and sentences, and seeks to analyze, catalogue and describe that data and that language. Descriptive linguistics is about describing languages rather than about constructing theories and models. It must, of course, use categories of description, but these arise inductively from a consideration of the language data rather than deductively from the axioms of a theory.

In many ways, descriptive linguistics is the successor to 'traditional grammar', as it used to be taught in schools. And it is ironic that, while in recent years great advances have been made in the description of contemporary English, the education system in Britain no longer demands that pupils should be acquainted with the nature and structure of their mother tongue. In the seventies a number of significant reference works have been published, distilling the latest knowledge about the English language, among them the *Grammar of contemporary English* by R Quirk, S Greenbaum, G Leech and J Svartvik, published by Longman in 1972.

This present book is aimed at those wishing to discover the techniques and insights of linguistics as applied to the description of the contemporary English language. Such persons might be students in further or higher education undertaking a course in linguistics or English language, without any school background in language analysis. Or they might be teachers or advanced learners of English as a Foreign Language, seeking the beginnings of a systematic linguistic description of modern English. Or they might be interested lay people wishing to know what this still relatively new science of linguistics has to say about the nature of the language they speak.

The book is divided into three sections, dealing with *Sounds* (ie pronunciation), *Structures* (ie grammar) and *Words* (ie vocabulary and meaning). The terminology used is, much of it, derived from traditional grammar, and it relates directly to that found in *A Grammar of contemporary English* and similar works. Each chapter presents a framework of analysis for the point being discussed, and is provided with an exercise, to give practice in applying the analytical techniques presented in the chapter. Solutions to the exercises are given in a key at the end. The aim of the book is to show how linguistic analysis and description is done and to lead the reader to make his own analyses. It is intended that the book may be used self-instructionally, or it could be used by a teacher. And it is hoped that after working through the book the reader will then be able to make practical analyses of any English sentence or text himself—with the aid of the reference works cited in the *Conclusion*.

Part One: Sounds

1. Making sounds

Speaking and writing

We can transmit our language in two ways: either by speaking or by writing. We are all conscious of what writing involves: the use of a pen or pencil in our hands, the making of special marks (letters) on paper. But we are not at all conscious of what speaking involves. It involves sound coming out of our mouths. But how is that sound produced? And how does it relate to the letters that we write? After all it is the same language, whether we speak it or write it.

The reason we are more conscious of writing is because we had to be taught how to write, how to hold the pencil correctly, how to shape the letters so that they could be recognized by someone else. But we learned to speak on our mother's knee. No one told us how to make the right sounds, what to do with our tongues or our lips. All natural languages have been transmitted by speech, but not all by writing. And all normal healthy people have learned to speak their language in childhood, but not all have learned to write. In this sense speech is prior to writing and characteristic of us as human beings.

When we speak we use over half of our bodies to do so, from the diaphragm, situated below the lungs, to the mouth and nose in our faces. Speech is quite simply a column of air, that originates in the lungs, and is modified in various ways before its passage through the lips, and so out of the mouth and into the air. Like any other sound, speech is the vibration of the the air to make sound waves. In this case the vibration, and the characteristics of the sound waves are determined by the human vocal organs.

What we have just described is the most usual basis of speech, ie **egressive** lung air—air originating in the lungs and passing outwards. It is also possible to speak while breathing in, with **ingressive** lung air. We sometimes speak like this in moments of tension, but it is not a normal way to produce speech sounds. However, ingressive mouth air sounds, produced when drawing air into the mouth but not into the lungs, do occur. For English speakers the **tut-tut** sound is made like this, and in some languages such sounds are regularly used. Egressive mouth air sounds also occur; for English speakers blowing a raspberry or giving a kiss are sounds of this kind. But for articulating the sounds of English words egressive lung air is virtually always used in normal English speech.

Vocal cords

As air is expelled from the lungs, it passes up the windpipe (trachea) and into the larynx (see *Figure 1*). In the larynx is found the glottis, the passage between the vocal cords (or vocal folds). Here the air coming from the lungs receives its first

3

major modification. The vocal cords, despite their name, are not to be imagined like strings of a guitar or piano. They are a pair of fleshy, lip-like membranes, that are hinged at the front and may be moved together or apart in order to impede or allow the passage of air through the glottis.

The action of the vocal cords (ie the state of the glottis) determines whether a sound being produced is voiced or voiceless. When the vocal cords are brought close together, but not shut tightly, the air escaping from the lungs causes them to

Figure 1: The vocal organs

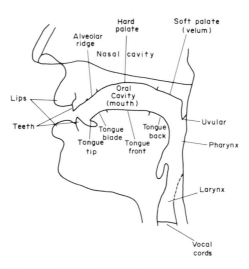

vibrate: this is called voicing, and a sound produced while the vocal cords are vibrating is a voiced sound. When the vocal cords are apart, no vibration occurs, and sounds produced with the glottis in this state are voiceless sounds. This is also the state of the glottis for normal breathing. The vibratory action of the vocal cords may be easily demonstrated by blocking up the ears and producing alternately an **s** and a **z** sound. The **s** is a voiceless sound and the **z** a voiced sound. The articulation of the latter should induce a buzzing sensation.

There are two further possible states of the glottis, which are both of marginal interest to the production of speech. One is when the vocal cords are brought tightly together and the glottis is completely closed. We do this when we are lifting heavy objects, and it occurs in speech as a momentary action, in the production of the 'glottal stop', familiar from the Cockney pronunciation of the **tt** in *butter*. The other state of the glottis is intermediate between vibrating and completely open: the vocal cords are brought together, but not sufficiently for vibration to occur. This is the state of the glottis associated with whispering.

Summarizing, there are four possible states of the glottis:
1. *Open and relaxed,* used for normal breathing and making voiceless sounds;
2. *Vibrating,* used for making voiced sounds;
3. *Completely shut,* used for making the glottal stop;

4. *Close together* but not vibrating, used for whispering.
Only the first two are of importance in the description of speech sounds, giving us the categories of **voiceless** and **voiced** sounds. A speech sound must belong to one or the other of these categories, and this is determined by the state of the glottis at the time of its production.

Oral and nasal sounds

As the column of air passes beyond the glottis, through the pharynx, there are two possible ways of escape from the face: either through the mouth, or through the nose. At the back of the mouth, as an extension of the roof, is the soft palate, or velum. This is under muscular control and may at any time be in one of two positions: either raised, or lowered. If the soft palate is raised, the passage through the nose is blocked and air may escape only through the mouth. If the soft palate is lowered, the passage through the nose is free, and air may escape both through the nose and through the mouth. Sounds produced with the soft palate lowered are **nasal** or nasalized sounds. Sounds produced with the soft palate raised and air escaping only through the mouth are called **oral** sounds. Indeed we assume that sounds are oral unless we use the term nasal or nasalized. The difference between oral and nasal sounds may be illustrated from the word *sudden*. In a normal, fairly rapid pronunciation of this word, the final two sounds are **dn**. The only respect in which these sounds differ from each other is that **d** is an oral sound and **n** is a nasal sound. If you monitor your pronunciation carefully you should be able to feel the action of the soft palate in the transition from **d** to **n**, ie from a raised to a lowered position.

The function of the soft palate is, then, either to allow or not to allow the passage of air through the nose. When it is lowered it does not restrict the escape of air through the mouth. However the escape of air through the mouth may be restricted in other ways, and air may be escaping only through the nose. For example, in the pronunciation of **m**, air cannot escape from the mouth because the lips are tightly shut, so that the escape of air is only through the nasal cavity.

The most complex modifications of the column of air that originated in the lungs take place in the mouth. Here we are concerned with two aspects of articulation: firstly, the **manner of articulation**; and secondly the **place of articulation**. The manner of articulation refers to the way in which a sound is made, and the place refers to the position in the mouth at which the sound is made. A number of sounds made in different ways may be made at the same position.

Manner of articulation

With manner of articulation we first of all make a broad distinction between sounds that are produced without any obstruction in the mouth, and those that are made with some kind of obstruction. The former we call **vowels** and the latter **consonants**. The differing quality of vowel sounds is determined by the openness of the mouth, the configuration of the tongue and the shape of the lips. The quality of consonant sounds is determined by the kind of obstruction to the passage of air (or **closure**), as well as by the place of articulation.

Figure 2: Near closure for *s*

Complete closure

A number of kinds of closure may be identified. First there is the **complete closure**, when a total obstruction is made to the flow of air. When the soft palate is raised and air is prevented from escaping through the nose, air-pressure will build up behind the obstruction, and may then be released with an explosion. Sounds produced in this way are called **plosive** sounds (or sometimes stops). Such a sound in English is the initial **b** in **bin**. Here the complete closure is made by the two lips. Obviously the closure, the build up of air-pressure, and the plosion are momentary activities; but they are all three stages in the articulation of plosive sounds. If, with a complete closure, the soft palate is lowered, then air may escape through the nose. Sounds made in this way are called **nasal** sounds, eg **m** in English *man*, where the closure is again made by the lips.

Figure 3: Complete closure for *g*

Near closure

A second kind is a **near-closure**. Here the air is allowed to escape, but not freely. The escaping air causes friction at the point of near-closure, and the sounds produced in this way are called **fricative** sounds. Such a sound in English is the initial **v** of *van*. Here the near-closure is between the bottom lip and the top front teeth, with friction resulting.

Laterals

A third kind is made with the front of the tongue forming a complete closure, but with the air being allowed to escape over the sides of the tongue. Sounds produced in this way are called **lateral** sounds, since the air escapes laterally. Now, the air escape may be completely free, as in the case of the initial **1** of English *lid*, or the sides of the tongue may be raised, so that air escapes only with friction, as in the initial **11** of Welsh **Llan-**. This latter sound is called a **lateral fricative**.

Intermittent closure

A fourth kind is an **intermittent closure**. In making sounds with an intermittent closure, a complete closure is made very quickly and repeated several times. Such a sound is the **rolled r**, sometimes heard with an emphatic (or Scottish) pronunciation of **r** in, for example, *red*. Here the intermittent closure is between the tip of the tongue and the back of the upper front teeth. An intermittent closure may, however, involve only one such closure, in which case it is called a **flapped** sound, sometimes heard when **r** occurs between vowels eg in *very*.

Near closures without friction

A fifth and final kind is a near-closure, like the second kind, but without friction. The articulators come close together, but not close enough for friction to occur. These sounds are called **frictionless continuant** sounds. Such a sound is the initial **w** in *wet*. Here the near-closure occurs between the two lips. These sounds could be classed as vowels, since they are made without any obstruction to the air-flow through the mouth, but they are usually regarded as consonants, at least as far as English is concerned, because they act like consonants in all other respects, especially in syllable and word structure.

These, then, are the categories that we use to describe the manner of articulation of sounds. There is first of all the broad distinction between vowels and consonants, and then among consonants we distinguish between plosives, nasals, fricatives, laterals, rolls and flaps, and frictionless continuants.

Place of articulation

Now let us consider the place of articulation of sounds. From what has been said about the distinction between vowels and consonants, it will be clear that consonants are easier to describe for place of articulation than vowels, since it is possible to feel where the obstruction is taking place in the mouth. Nevertheless, vowel sounds may be described in terms of their place of articulation.

Vowels

Two sets of categories are relevant to this description. The first involves the openness of the mouth and height of the tongue, for which the categories are **close, half-close, half-open, open** (an alternative corresponding set of categories is also sometimes used: **high, mid-high, mid-low, low**). The second involves the general configuration of the tongue and the area of the mouth in which the sound is made, the categories here are **front, central, back**. A third set of categories is relevant to the description of vowel sounds, involving the shape of the lips; the categories are

rounded and **spread** (also referred to as unrounded). Illustrating from English, the vowel sound in *beat*, represented by the letters **ea**, is a close front vowel with spread lips; the vowel sound in *boot*, represented by the letters **oo**, is a close back vowel with rounded lips.

Figure 4: Vowel Chart showing *ea* and *oo*

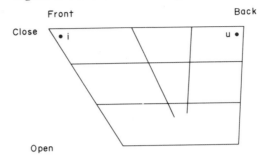

Consonants

In making consonant sounds, two parts of the mouth, or articulators, are involved. For the majority, one of these articulators is the tongue, or at least some part of the tongue. Since this is so, the label for tongue, (from Latin *lingua*), is not usually included in the description of the place of articulation of the sound.

We will begin our review of places of articulation at the front of the mouth. The

Figure 5: Bilabial *b*   **Figure 6:** Labio-dental *f*

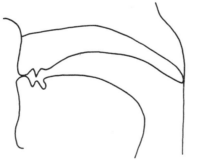 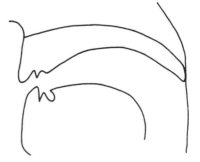

first place involves the two lips as articulators, and sounds made here are called **bilabial** sounds (from Latin *labium*). They may be illustrated from the initial **b** in *bit*, which is a bilabial plosive, or the initial **m** in *men*, which is a bilabial nasal. At the next place of articulation the bottom lip makes a closure with the top front teeth; these sounds are called **labio-dental** sounds. In English the initial **f** of *fun* is a labio-dental fricative.

The other consonant sounds all involve the tongue as one of the articulators. First, consonants are made by the articulation of the tip of the tongue and the back of the upper front teeth; these are called **dental** sounds (from Latin *dens*). In English the final sound in *teeth*, represented by the letters **th**, is a dental fricative. Next, a sound is made by the articulation of the tongue and the bony ridge just behind the upper front teeth. The part of the tongue used is that just behind the tip, called the blade,

Figure 7: Dental *th*

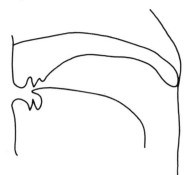

Figure 8: Alveolar *d*

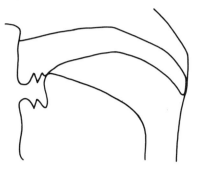

and the bony ridge is called the alveolar ridge, which gives the name to the sounds made in this position – **alveolar** sounds. In English the initial **d** of *din* is an alveolar plosive. The next area of the roof of the mouth, behind the alveolar ridge, is called the hard palate. An articulation occurs between the hard palate and the part of the

Figure 9: Palatal *y*

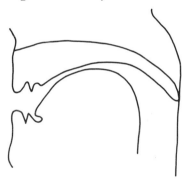

tongue behind the blade, called the front of the tongue. These sounds are called **palatal** sounds; in English the initial sound of *yes*, represented by the letter **y**, is a palatal frictionless continuant.

If you run your tongue over the roof of your mouth you will feel the hard palate being replaced by a soft area, called the soft palate or velum. There is an articulation between this area and the back of the tongue, making **velar** sounds: in English the initial **g** of *get* is a velar plosive. The velum extends into the uvula, the piece of flesh that you can see dangling at the back of your mouth when you look in a mirror. The uvula articulates with the back of the tongue to produce **uvular** sounds. In French the **r** sound is often a uvular roll, with the uvula making an intermittent closure against the back of the tongue. Moving further back in the mouth we come to the pharynx; it is possible for an articulation to occur between the back or root of the tongue and the pharynx, giving a **pharyngeal** sound. No such sounds occur in English or the European languages; they are typical, however, of Arabic. Proceeding beyond the pharynx we come to the glottis, where the position

Figure 10: Velar *g*

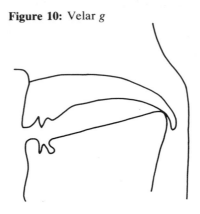

of the vocal cords may produce **glottal** sounds. We have mentioned the production of the glottal stop (the Cockney pronunciation of the **tt** in *butter*) by means of a complete closure in the glottis.

From this description of the possible places of articulation for speech sounds it will be clear that for purposes of description, the tongue is divided into a number of identifiable areas as is also the roof of the mouth. Beginning at the front end, the

Figure 11: Parts of the tongue and roof of the mouth

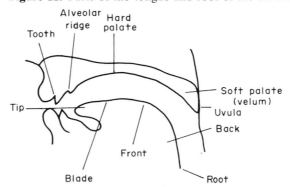

parts of the tongue that are distinguished are: tip, blade, front, back, root. The areas of the roof of the mouth are alveolar ridge, (hard) palate, velum (ie soft palate), uvula.

Describing speech sounds

In describing speech sounds there is a convention well worth following. When labelling a vowel sound, give first of all the category for height, then the one for the general area of the mouth, and then the one for the position of the lips. Thus, the vowel of *beat* is described as a close front spread vowel. Vowels are assumed to be voiced, ie articulated with the vocal cords vibrating, since this is predominantly the case. And in English, at any rate, there is no regular distinction to be made between voiced and voiceless vowels. In labelling consonant sounds however, voicing is important and is given first, then the place of articulation, and finally the manner of articulation. Thus, the **b** of *beat* is described as a voiced bilabial plosive, and the **f** of *fun* as a voiceless labio-dental fricative.

International Phonetic Alphabet

It will have become clear that the Roman alphabet, which we use for writing English, is by no means adequate for representing the diversity of speech sounds that we use for speaking English. The inadequacy becomes evident if we reflect that there are over 40 distinguishable speech sounds in English, while our alphabet contains only 26 symbols. To make the point more concrete, consider that we have to use a pair of letters (**th**) to represent the single voiceless dental fricative sound at the end of *teeth*. Moreover, this same pair of letters also serves to represent the voiced dental fricative sound, as found at the beginning of *then*. So in representing speech we make use of the International Phonetic Alphabet, developed by the International Phonetic Association. This alphabet is based on the Roman alphabet, but with the addition of symbols from other sources. We shall be introducing the symbols that are necessary for representing English speech sounds in the following chapters, and the complete alphabet is given on page 151.

Exercise 1

Make a description of the following speech sounds in the way recommended eg the **b** of *beat*—voiced bilabial plosive; the **ea** of *beat*—close front spread vowel.
1. the **t** of *beat*
2. the **v** of *van*
3. the **k** of *kiss*
4. the **th** of *thin*
5. the **n** of *now*
6. the **a** of *bath*
7. the **p** of *pin*
8. the **ee** of *seed*
9. the **o** of *bottle*
10. the **l** of *like*
11. the **g** of *go*
12. the **z** of *zoo*

2. English consonants

In the previous chapter we defined consonants as those speech sounds which are produced with some kind of closure in the mouth, restricting the escape of air. And we distinguished among consonants according to the place in the mouth that the closure occurs (place of articulation) and according to the kind of closure made (manner of articulation). These factors, along with the state of the glottis (voicing), determine the kind of consonant sound that is produced. We shall now take each of these classes of consonants in turn, discover which sounds are used in English, and introduce the phonetic symbol for each sound from the International Phonetic Alphabet.

Fricatives

The largest group of consonants in English comprises the **fricatives**, sounds that involve a near-closure with friction resulting between the articulators. In most cases there is a voiced and a voiceless fricative occurring at each place of articulation.

Bilabial fricatives, where the friction occurs between the two lips, have symbols taken from the Greek alphabet: for the voiceless bilabial fricative the symbol is ɸ,

Figure 12: Bilabial fricative

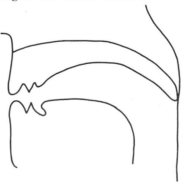

and for the voiced bilabial fricative β. These sounds do not regularly occur in English, except in certain contexts as variant sounds for labio-dental fricatives (see Chapter 5).

The **labio-dental fricatives** have the familiar symbols f and v for the voiceless and voiced variety respectively. Friction occurs between the lower lip and the upper front teeth. These sounds occur regularly in English words, in all positions, eg initially in *feign/vain*; medially in *referee/reverie*; finally in *life/live*. When the phonetic symbol is a familiar one, as in this case, it should not be assumed that when the corresponding letter occurs it always represents the sound that the phonetic symbol stands for. So, in the case of the letter *f* for example, the word written *of* is in fact pronounced with a voiced labio-dental fricative as the final sound, ie represented by the phonetic symbol v.

Figure 13: Dental fricative

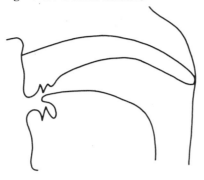

In producing **dental fricatives** the friction occurs between the tongue tip and the back of the front teeth. For some speakers the tongue tip actually protrudes between top and bottom teeth, and these sounds are sometimes called interdental fricatives. One symbol is taken from the Greek alphabet: for the voiceless dental fricative the symbol is θ; and for the voiced dental fricative—ð, which is a specially invented symbol. These sounds occur in all positions in English words, eg *thief/this; lethal/leather; cloth/clothe.*

Figure 14: Alveolar fricative

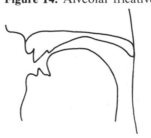

The **alveolar fricatives** have familiar symbols, s for the voiceless alveolar fricative, and z for the voiced alveolar fricative. Again, it should be noted that not all occurrences of the letter *s* are voiceless alveolar fricatives, ie symbolized phonetically by s; eg *rise* has a voiced alveolar fricative as its final sound, represented phonetically by z. With alveolar fricatives the friction is between the tongue tip or blade and the alveolar ridge. But they differ from dental fricatives not only in place of articulation, but also in the shape that the tongue takes up in the articulation of the sound. With alveolar fricatives in English the tongue is shaped so that there is a groove down the centre line along which the air passes, whereas with dental fricatives the tongue is relatively flat with only a narrow slit. So s and z are **groove fricatives** in English, while θ and ð are **slit fricatives.** The alveolar fricatives occur in all positions in English words, although z is not common initially: *seal/zeal, racer/razor, lace/laze.*

Figure 15: Palato-alveolar fricative

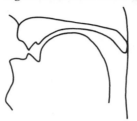

Further back in the mouth we come to the pair of **palato-alveolar fricatives.** Friction occurs between the tongue front and the hard palate, but at the same time the tongue tip is raised towards the alveolar ridge. These sounds are symbolized by ʃ for the voiceless palato-alveolar fricative, and ʒ for the voiced palato-alveolar fricative. They occur in all positions in English words, eg, *ship/gigolo, fission/vision, rush/rouge.* But the voiced palato-alveolar fricative is of very restricted occurrence initially and finally, found only in words borrowed from French; and there is a tendency in some people's speech to replace the voiced palato-alveolar fricative in these positions with the voiced affricate (see below).

Palatal fricatives do not occur in English. Of the **velar fricatives** only the voiceless member occurs, and then in only a few words borrowed from other languages. The velar fricative is produced with friction between the tongue back and the soft palate, and the voiceless member is symbolized by x. It occurs in the Scottish pronunciation of *loch*, and in some German names, eg of the composer *Bach*.

The only other fricative to note in English is the **glottal fricative**, which occurs only as a voiceless sound. It is represented by the symbol h. This consonant occurs mainly initially, although it is also sometimes found medially, eg *head/ahead, hill/uphill.* It is sometimes discounted as a consonant by phoneticians of English. In articulating the h the mouth takes up a configuration for the following vowel sound, and for this reason it is considered to be a **voiceless onset** for the vowel which follows. But for practical recognition and transcription purposes it is useful to regard it as a separate sound, and we shall call it a **voiceless glottal fricative**, symbolized by h.

Figure 16: Velar fricative

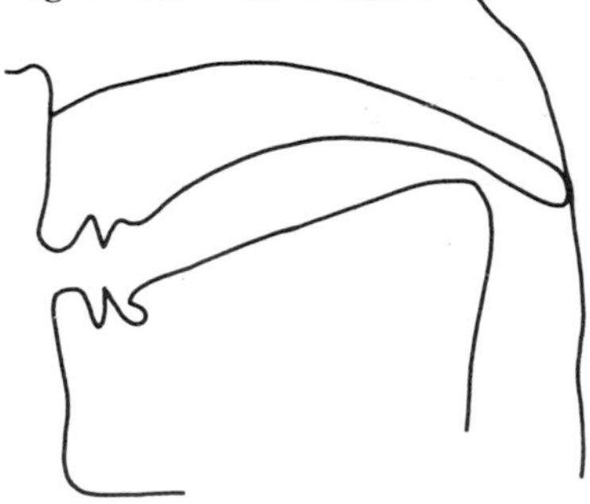

Plosives

Plosive consonants in English involve a complete closure in the mouth, a raised velum preventing escape of air through the nasal cavity, and plosion after the release of the closure.

Figure 17: Bilabial plosive

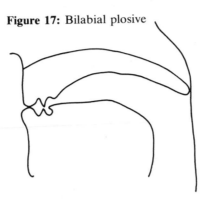

Bilabial plosives occur commonly in English and are represented by the familiar symbols p and b, for the voiceless bilabial plosive and the voiced bilabial plosive respectively. They are found in all positions in English words, eg *pear/bear, chapel/cable, rope/robe.*

Figure 18: Alveolar plosive

Figure 19: Velar plosive

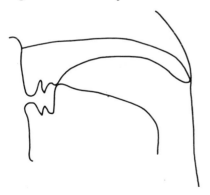
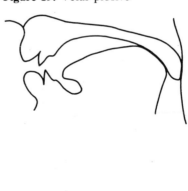

The **alveolar plosives** are made with a closure between the tongue blade, or sometimes tongue tip, and the alveolar ridge. They are represented by the familiar symbols t and d, for voiceless alveolar plosive and voiced alveolar plosive respectively. They occur frequently in all positions in English words, eg *train/drain, writer/rider, mat/mad.*

A final pair of plosives in English is made at the velar place of articulation, involving a closure between the tongue back and the soft palate. The voiceless **velar plosive** is symbolized by k and the voiced velar plosive by g. Like the other plosives they are found commonly in all positions in English words, eg *cane/gain, package/baggage, rick/rig.*

In many cases the voiceless plosives in English are articulated with aspiration accompanying the release phase of pronunciation. This means that when plosion occurs, a puff of air accompanies it. So we talk about **aspirated** and **unaspirated** voiceless plosives, and aspirated voiceless plosives are symbolized p^h, t^h, k^h. The aspiration of voiceless plosives in English is a more-or-less phenomenon rather than an either-or one; that is to say, there are a number of degrees of aspiration rather than aspiration versus non-aspiration. Strong aspiration is typical when voiceless plosives occur initially, and a complete absence of aspiration typically occurs when voiceless plosives follow s, cf *pin/spin, tin/stint, kill/skill.* A lighter aspiration is often present when voiceless plosives occur medially or finally, eg *hopper/hope, latter/~ late, packer/pack.*

There is one further plosive that we should include—the glottal plosive, or **glottal stop**, that we mentioned in Chapter 1. It is not really a plosive, in that no observable plosion occurs; hence 'stop', the alternative name for plosive, seems more appropriate in this instance. Only a voiceless glottal plosive occurs; it is represented by the symbol ?. Apart from its widespread use in Cockney and some other accents, its occurrence in English speech is restricted to special uses. It may be heard in the pronunciation of words where two vowels follow each other but belong to separate syllables, eg *co-operate, re-action.* Here a glottal stop is often used to separate the two vowels. It may also be heard on occasions as a reinforcement of the articulation of a final voiceless plosive, eg in *leap* or *leak.*

Affricates

One pair of sounds in English is related to both plosives and fricatives: the **palato-alveolar affricates**. The voiceless palato-alveolar affricate may be illustrated by the initial and final sounds in *church*, and the voiced by the initial and final sounds in *judge.* Affricates involve a complete closure, as for plosives, but the release phase is not with plosion but with friction. In the case of the palato-alveolar affricates the closure is made with the tongue blade and front at the alveolar ridge and hard palate area, and the release is by means of a palato-alveolar fricative. These sounds are symbolized by tʃ for the voiceless palato-alveolar affricate, and by

Figure 20: Palato-alveolar affricate

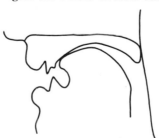

dʒ for the voiced palato-alveolar affricate. They occur in all positions in English words, eg *chin/gin, riches/ridges, lunch/lunge.*

Nasals

Like plosives, **nasals** involve a complete closure in the mouth; but unlike for plosives, the soft palate is lowered so that air may escape through the nose. Nasals, unlike plosives, but like fricatives, are continuant sounds. This means that their articulation may continue for as long as the person speaking can find breath: compare mmm, fff, p. In English, nasal consonants are normally voiced; voiceless nasals do sometimes occur in some contexts, but they are then variants of normal voiced nasals, and may be ignored for our purposes.

English has a **bilabial nasal**, represented by the familiar symbol m, which occurs in all positions in English words, eg *mind, limit, rhyme*. The **labio-dental nasal**, involving a closure between bottom lip and upper teeth, is represented by the symbol ɱ. This is not a regular sound in English, occurring only as a variant of the bilabial m or the alveolar nasal n before labio-dental fricatives, eg in *symphony* and in *infant*. And then it occurs really only in fairly rapid speech. It will be mentioned again in Chapter 5.

As already implied, English has an **alveolar nasal**, represented by the familiar symbol n, which occurs in all positions in English words, eg *night, lantern, line*. Finally, English has a **velar nasal**, involving a closure between the back of the tongue and the soft palate. It is represented by the symbol ŋ, and is of restricted occurrence, never being found initially. It occurs frequently before a velar plosive, and in some accents of English, eg in the Midlands, it is always followed by a velar plosive. In other accents it may occur finally as well as medially, eg *linger, tongue, singer*.

Laterals

Like nasals, the **lateral** consonants are also continuant sounds: there is a complete closure, but air escapes over the side of the tongue. In English laterals are normally voiced, although there is a voiceless variant that regularly occurs in a particular context and which will be discussed later (Chapter 4). The only lateral occurring in English is the **alveolar lateral**, represented by the familiar symbol l. It is found in all positions in English words, eg *late, filler, tail*. In fact, there is a marked difference in quality between the alveolar lateral in initial position and that in final position. The difference arises from the configuration of the body of the tongue in the mouth: for the alveolar lateral in final position, the back of the tongue is raised towards the soft palate, and it is said to be velarized. The velarized alveolar lateral is symbolized by ɫ:

Figure 21: Alveolar lateral – non-velarized and velarized

compare *leaf/feel, late/tail*. The details of the contexts in which the two varieties occur will be discussed in Chapter 4.

Frictionless continuants

Last in our review of English consonants we come to the class of **frictionless continuants**, the sounds involving a near-closure in the mouth but without friction. The normal English r sound is a **post-alveolar frictionless continuant**: a near-closure is made between the tongue blade and the area just behind the alveolar ridge. It is represented in the International Phonetic Alphabet by the symbol ɹ, but for purposes of broad transcription (see Chapter 4) it may be more convenient to use the usual orthographic r symbol. It is of restricted occurrence in English, not normally being found in final position eg *run, free, furrow*. The orthographic symbol appears frequently in final position in English spelling, but careful observation will reveal that in British English it is not normally pronounced in that position, eg *car, more, bear, farm*, although it is pronounced here in many American accents. Other kinds of r sound are also found in English speech and will be discussed later (Chapter 4). The post-alveolar frictionless continuant is reckoned to be the normal English r sound. It is usually voiced, although a voiceless variant does occur in some contexts (see Chapter 4).

Two further sounds are included among the frictionless continuants, although they are sometimes also called **semi-vowels**. They have similarity with particular vowel sounds of English, and were it not for the fact that they pattern like consonants in the structure of English words and syllables, they would be counted as these vowels.

One is the **bilabial frictionless continuant**, represented by the familiar symbol w, which is similar to the close back rounded vowel, as in *boot*. This occurs in initial and medial positions, eg *wet, tower*. But in final positions its occurrence in spelling is usually considered to be a close back rounded vowel.

The other vowel-like consonant sound is the **palatal frictionless continuant**, where the near-closure is between the tongue front and the hard palate. It is represented by the symbol j, and it is similar to a close front spread vowel as in *beat*. The occurrence of the palatal frictionless continuant is restricted: it is found in initial position, and in initial consonant combinations after certain consonants, eg *yet, beauty* (bj), *queue* (kj). Both these frictionless continuants are normally voiced.

By way of summary the consonants of English are set out in a chart below. Place of articulation is indicated across the top of the chart, and manner of articulation down the left-hand side. If a particular kind of consonant has a voiceless and a voiced variant, then two symbols appear in the relevant box in the order voiceless followed by voiced. Consonants that occur only as variants of other regularly occurring sounds have been omitted from the chart.

Figure 22: English consonants

	Bilabial	Labio-Dental	Dental	Alveolar	Palato-Alveolar	Palatal	Velar	Glottal
Fricative		f v	θ ð	s z	ʃ ʒ			h
Plosive	p b			t d			k g	
Affricate					tʃ dʒ			
Nasal	m			n			ŋ	
Lateral				l				
Frictionless Continuant	w			ɹ		j		

Exercise 2

Transcribe the following English words in the symbols of the International Phonetic Alphabet charted in *Figure 22* to represent their pronunciation. Since every word has a vowel sound, a number of vowel symbols will be needed. The following vowels have been used in the words listed: i as in *peep*, ɪ as in *pit*, ɛ as in *bet*, and ɑ as in the educated southern English pronunciation of *path*.

eg *then* ðɛn; *jar* dʒɑ; *lick* lɪk

1. shed	2. teeth	3. chart
4. detest	5. jet	6. guard
7. these	8. barge	9. vase
10. chef	11. peach	12. thieve
13. yeast	14. green	15. Mars
16. wealth	17. heel	18. wrench
19. crease	20. charge	21. shriek
22. fling	23. stink	24. yield

3. English vowels

In Chapter 1 we defined vowels as sounds which are made without any kind of closure or impediment to the escape of air through the mouth. Because there is no contact or near-contact of articulators, vowel sounds are more difficult to describe than are consonants. But, as with many consonants, the tongue is crucial in determining the quality of vowel sounds, and it is the differing configurations of the tongue in the mouth that cause the varying qualities.

As we mentioned in Chapter 1, there are three parameters by which we describe vowel sounds: firstly, the height of the tongue or openness of the mouth; secondly, the area of the mouth having the highest part of the tongue or the general area of the mouth in which the vowel is made; and thirdly, the shape of the lips. The first of these gives us the categories **close, half-close, half-open** and **open**; the second the categories **front, central**, and **back**; and the third the categories **rounded** and **spread**. Vowel sounds are, of course, normally voiced, so that voicing is not relevant for their description.

Before we look at the English vowels in detail we should mention a broad distinction to be made among vowel sounds between **pure vowels** and **diphthongs**. This is particularly relevant for English, since the proportion of diphthongs is unusually large. Pure vowels are made with the mouth taking up a single position during the articulation. In the case of diphthongs the configuration of the mouth changes in the course of the articulation of the vowel sound. As we shall see, diphthongs can be described in terms of the pure vowel from which the articulation starts, and the pure vowel in whose direction the articulation moves.

Pure vowels

First of all, we shall consider the pure vowels. In English, pure vowels are made in all three areas of the mouth—front, central and back.

Front vowels

In the front area English has four vowels; all are made with spread lips. Two of the front vowels are in the close area. One is the **close front spread** vowel found in *beat* or *sheep* and symbolized by i, so these words would be transcribed phonetically as /bit/ and /ʃip/. The other is a more open and a more central close front vowel, usually described as a **lowered and centralized close front spread** vowel. It is represented by the symbol ɪ, and it occurs in *bit* /bɪt/ and *ship* /ʃɪp/.

English has no vowel at precisely either the half-close or the half-open position, but one mid way between the two. This is usually described as a **mid front spread** vowel. It is sometimes symbolized by e, which is the International Phonetic Alphabet symbol for a half-close front spread vowel, but it is more usually symbolized by ɛ, the IPA symbol for a half-open front spread vowel, and this is the symbol we shall be using. This vowel occurs in *bet* /bɛt/ and *fetch* /fɛtʃ/.

The other English front vowel is in the open area, but it is not completely open: it is somewhere between half-open and open, although it is usually described as an **open front spread** vowel. However, the IPA symbol for an open front spread vowel (a) is not used, but rather the symbol æ. It occurs in *bat* /bæt/ and *catch* /kætʃ/.

Back vowels

In the back area of the mouth we can recognize five vowels in English. Four of them are made with rounded lips and one with spread lips. There are also two vowels in English that fall in the close back area. One is the **close back rounded** vowel, as found in *boot* and *tool* and symbolized by u, so these words will be transcribed phonetically as /but/ and /tul/. The other is a more open and more central variety, usually described as a **lowered and centralized close back rounded** vowel. It is represented by the symbol ʊ and occurs in (southern British pronunciations of) *book* /bʊk/ and *put* /pʊt/.

As in the case of front vowels, English has no vowels at precisely half-close and half-open back positions. There is one vowel somewhere between the two, probably nearer to half-open than half-close. The IPA symbol for a half-close back rounded vowel (o) is sometimes used to symbolize it, but more usually the IPA symbol for a half-open back rounded vowel is used, ɔ. It may be described as a **mid back rounded** vowel and it occurs in *bought* /bɔt/ and *law* /lɔ/.

In the open back area two vowels are found in English, one made with rounded lips, the other with spread lips. The open back rounded vowel is, like its front counterpart, not completely open, but somewhere between half-open and open. Nevertheless, the IPA symbol for an **open back rounded** vowel is used to represent it, ɒ. This vowel occurs in *hot* /hɒt/ and *moss* /mɒs/. The open back spread vowel is completely open but not completely back: it tends towards the central position. The IPA symbol for an **open back spread** vowel is used to represent it, ɑ, and it occurs in *farm* /fɑm/ and *cart* /kɑt/.

Central vowels

We come now to the final group of pure vowels, those made in the central area of the mouth. There are three vowels produced in this area in English, all with spread lips. One of these central vowels is in the open area, but like æ and ɒ in fact mid-way between half-open and open, although it is described as an **open central spread** vowel. It is represented by the IPA symbol for a half-open back spread vowel, namely ʌ, and it occurs in (the southern British pronunciation of) *but* /bʌt/ and *some* /sʌm/.

The other two central vowels in English are both **mid central spread** vowels, that is mid-way between half-close and half-open. These sounds may be illustrated by the vowel in *bird*, represented by the symbol ɜ, and the final vowel in *father*, represented by the symbol ə. The latter sound is often referred to as the **schwa** vowel; it occurs in English only in unstressed syllables and has a generally lax articulation. By contrast the ɜ vowel occurs in stressed syllables, and is generally longer in duration than the schwa vowel. They may be further illustrated by *loser* /luzə/, *ahead* /əhɛd/, *girl* /gɜl/, *first* /fɜst/.

This completes our description of the twelve English pure vowels. If you do not speak with a southern British accent, you may have found that some of the illustrations given did not match your pronunciation of the words. Indeed, some Midland and Northern speakers may find it difficult to discover a word in their speech that contains an open central spread vowel (ʌ). The differences in English accents are due to a considerable extent to the vowel sounds, and in two ways. Vowel sounds differ among accents in their quality; for example, in some accents the mid back rounded vowel is considerably more open in articulation than described here, eg in *caught* /kɔt/. And secondly, vowel sounds differ among accents in the words in which they occur; for example, most Northerners and some Midlanders will use a lowered and centralized close back rounded vowel (ʊ) in *but* rather than an open central spread vowel (ʌ). It is impossible to do justice to the variety of British English accents in a work of this kind, not to mention American, Australian and other accents. So, transcriptions will be given as representing southern British pronunciation, and the reader will be left to determine what the transcription will be for his own accent.

The vowel chart

So far we have characterized English vowel sounds by means of a descriptive label such as 'close front spread vowel', etc. Phoneticians also use another means of characterization: the vowel sounds are plotted on a vowel chart. This is a representation of the human mouth (in a squared out form!) and the peripheral points constitute a set of ideal sounds (called **cardinal vowels**) against which the sounds actually occurring in a language are compared and their points plotted on the chart. The IPA symbols are those given to the cardinal vowels. The chart of the pure vowels of southern British English is as shown below:

Figure 23: English vowels

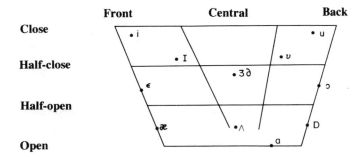

Diphthongs

Let us now consider the diphthongs of English, of which eight are usually recognized. They may be divided into three groups according to the vowel towards which the articulation of the diphthong moves. In the case of three diphthongs the articulation moves towards a lowered and centralized close front spread vowel (ɪ); in the case of two it moves towards a lowered and centralized close back rounded vowel (ʊ); and in the case of the remaining three it moves towards the unstressed mid central spread vowel (ə).

ɪ *diphthongs*

Taking each of these groups in turn, we begin with that in which the diphthong tends towards ɪ.

One of the diphthongs in this group begins with a half-close front spread vowel, so it is represented by the symbol eɪ. The beginning point of this diphthong is then more close than the articulation of the mid front spread pure vowel of English (ɛ). This diphthong is found in *late* /leɪt/ and *blame* /bleɪm/.

A second diphthong in this group begins with an open front spread vowel and is represented by the symbol aɪ. The beginning point is more open than the articulation of the English pure vowel described as open front spread (æ). It occurs in *sight* /saɪt/ and *mice* /maɪs/.

The third diphthong in this group begins with a half-open back rounded vowel; it is sometimes represented by the symbol ɔɪ and sometimes by the symbol ɒɪ, since the half-open position is mid way between the English pure vowel symbolized ɔ and the vowel symbolized ɒ, the former being mid way between half-close and half-open, and the latter mid way between half-open and open. We shall be using the latter symbol, ɒɪ. This diphthong occurs in *soil* /sɒɪl/ and *boy* /bɒɪ/.

ʊ *diphthongs*

The second group of diphthongs comprises those tending towards ʊ.

The first in this group starts with the unstressed mid central spread vowel and is represented by the symbol əʊ. This diphthong occurs in *home* /həʊm/ and in *boat* /bəʊt/.

The other in this group starts with an open central spread vowel, a vowel which is slightly more central than the English pure vowel described as open back spread; and in fact the symbol used for this pure vowel is also used in the symbolization of the diphthong, ɑʊ. This occurs in *house* /hɑʊs/ and *owl* /ɑʊl/.

It will be noticed that in making both the diphthongs of this group, not only is a change in the shape and height of the tongue involved, but also a change in the shape of the lips, moving from a spread vowel to a rounded one.

ə diphthongs

The third group of diphthongs tends towards the mid central spread vowel ə.

First there is a diphthong beginning with the lowered and centralized close front spread vowel and represented by the symbol ɪə. This occurs in *fierce* /fɪəs/ and *clear* /klɪə/.

A second in this group begins with a half-open front spread vowel, that is with a vowel more open than the pure vowel described as mid front spread. The symbol of this pure vowel is used in the diphthong and is the IPA symbol for a half-open front spread vowel. So the diphthong is represented by the symbol ɛə and occurs in *scarce* /skɛəs/ and *fair* /fɛə/.

The remaining diphthong of this group begins with a lowered and centralized close back rounded vowel and is represented by the symbol ʊə. It occurs in *cruel* /krʊəl/ and *pure* /pjʊə/.

The eight diphthongs of English may be plotted on a vowel chart:

Figure 24: English diphthongs

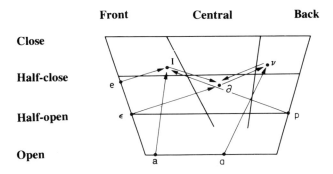

Exercise 3

Make a transcription of the pronunciation of the following English words, using the symbols discussed. The *Key* will give a representation of a southern British pronunciation; you may like to also consider what the transcription should be in your own accent.
eg *humble* /hʌmbəl/, *lathe* /leɪð/, *badge* /bædʒ/

1. caught	2. another	3. faint
4. sock	5. bag	6. cover
7. turn	8. fuel	9. count
10. look	11. catching	12. tile
13. large	14. beg	15. dozen
16. dirty	17. share	18. goal
19. food	20. flesh	21. fear
22. fall	23. morning	24. pleased
25. confess	26. moist	27. plain
28. salt	29. lurking	30. climb

Summary

As a summary of the last chapter and the present one, here is a list of the 44 sounds of English that we have identified and described. Each one is given with its symbol followed by its label.

Consonants

f   voiceless labio-dental fricative
v   voiced labio-dental fricative
θ   voiceless dental fricative
ð   voiced dental fricative
s   voiceless alveolar fricative
z   voiced alveolar fricative
ʃ   voiceless palato-alveolar fricative
ʒ   voiced palato-alveolar fricative
h   voiceless glottal fricative
p   voiceless bilabial plosive
b   voiced bilabial plosive
t   voiceless alveolar plosive
d   voiced alveolar plosive
k   voiceless velar plosive
g   voiced velar plosive
tʃ   voiceless palato-alveolar affricate
dʒ   voiced palato-alveolar affricate
m   bilabial nasal
n   alveolar nasal
ŋ   velar nasal
l   alveolar lateral
w   bilabial frictionless continuant
ɹ   post alveolar frictionless continuant
j   palatal frictionless continuant.

Vowels

i   close front spread vowel
ɪ   lowered and centralised close front spread vowel
ɛ   mid front spread vowel
æ   open front spread vowel
u   close back rounded vowel
ʊ   lowered and centralized close back rounded vowel
ɔ   mid back rounded vowel
ɒ   open back rounded vowel
ɑ   open back spread vowel
ɜ   mid central spread vowel
ə   unstressed mid central spread vowel
ʌ   open central spread vowel

eɪ   diphthong beginning with half-close front spread vowel, moving towards lowered and centralized close front spread vowel

aɪ   diphthong beginning with open front spread vowel, moving towards lowered and centralized close front spread vowel

ɒɪ   diphthong beginning with half-open back rounded vowel, moving towards lowered and centralized close front spread vowel

əʊ   diphthong beginning with unstressed mid central spread vowel, moving towards lowered and centralized close back rounded vowel

ɑʊ   diphthong beginning with open central spread vowel, moving towards lowered and centralized close back rounded vowel

ɪə   diphthong beginning with lowered and centralized close front spread vowel, moving towards unstressed mid central spread vowel

ɛə   dipthong beginning with half-open front spread vowel, moving towards unstressed mid central spread vowel

ʊə   diphthong beginning with lowered and centralized close back rounded vowel, moving towards unstressed mid central spread vowel.

Exercise 4

Make a transcription of the pronunciation of the following English words, using the symbols given.

1. playground	2. flexible	3. Chinese
4. drudgery	5. insinuation	6. pleasurable
7. blinkers	8. understate	9. search-warrant
10. blackmail	11. migration	12. frequency
13. robust	14. forceps	15. paranoia
16. birthday	17. cared-for	18. writhing
19. cure-all	20. overestimate	

4. Sounds and their variants

In the preceding chapters we have in general assumed that each sound that we perceive as a separate sound in English is transcribed by just one symbol: p sounds are transcribed by /p/, l sounds by /l/, and so on. At the same time we have also noticed that some such perceptually different sounds may, in different contexts, have different phonetic values. We have distinguished, for example, between a non-velarized and a velarized alveolar lateral (l and ł); and we have noticed aspirated and unaspirated varieties of voiceless plosives (eg pʰ and p). But in transcription we have not taken account of these finer differences, although we could have done. If we had done so, we should have produced a **narrow transcription** instead of the **broad** one we have been making.

Broad and narrow transcription

A broad transcription is one that only takes account of the sound differences that are important to distinguish words from each other in a language. The distinction between [pʰ] and [p] does not make a difference between words in English. If we substitute [p] for [pʰ] in [pʰɪn] we produce a peculiar pronunciation of *pin* but not a new word; similarly, if we substitute [pʰ] for [p] in [spɪn]. But the substitution of p for t does make a difference of word: *pin* /pɪn/ and *tin* /tɪn/ are different words in English. A narrow transcription attempts to represent more or less accurately the way in which a particular speaker pronounces his words. Obviously the amount of phonetic detail that may be represented can vary enormously; that is to say, there are degrees of narrowness of transcription, and a narrow transcription may be made for the pronunciation of a group of speakers, with a particular dialect or accent.

This distinction is, in fact, not merely a distinction between different kinds of transcription: it is also a distinction between different ways of looking at the sounds of a language. When the sound system of a language is viewed as a system of units for maintaining distinctions between units on a higher level of linguistic organization (ie words), we call the sounds **phonemes**. The sounds that people actually make when they speak are called **phones**. It is part of the task of phonology (or phonetics) to establish and describe the relationship between phones and phonemes in a language.

Phonemes and allophones

The phonologist starts with phones, the accurate phonetic transcription of the sounds that he hears speakers making. But it soon becomes clear that not all the distinctions made at this level are relevant for distinguishing words from each other. Or, to put it another way, native speakers do not perceive as distinct sounds all the phones that the phonologist has recorded. Several phones may, therefore, belong to the same phoneme; or a phoneme may have a number of variants, called **allophones**. In grouping phones together into phonemes, three criteria are used by the phonologist: complementary distribution, free variation, and phonetic similarity.

Complementary distribution

The criterion of **complementary distribution** states that if two or more phones occur in non-identical environments, then they may be members of the same phoneme. So, we find that for English the non-velarized alveolar lateral [l] occurs before vowels, while the velarized alveolar lateral [ł] occurs before consonants and at the ends of words. Their distribution in English words is complementary; they do not occur in the same environment. Hence these two 1-phones belong to the same phoneme. Or, we can say that the /l/ phoneme has two allophones: (1) [l] occurring before vowels; and (2) [ł] occurring before consonants and word-finally. From this statement you will notice the following convention: a broad transcription ie in terms of phonemes, is enclosed between slashed brackets / /; and a narrow transcription, ie in terms of phones, is enclosed between square brackets [ ]. Taking a contrary example, we find that the phone [pʰ] and the phone [tʰ] both occur in a number of identical environments eg *ton/pun, shop/shot, sipping/sitting*. Their distribution is, therefore, not complementary and they cannot be considered as belonging to the same phoneme.

Free variation

The criterion of **free variation** states that if two or more phones occur in the same environment, but without changing the word in which they occur, then they may belong to the same phoneme. So, in English, a word like *bid* is sometimes articulated with a fully voiced final alveolar consonant [d], and sometimes with a devoiced (voiceless) final consonant, represented by [d̥]. But whichever phone is used, the word is the same. These two phones, then, belong to the same phoneme. Or we can say that the phoneme /d/ has two allophones when it occurs word-finally: (1) [d], and (2) [d̥], which are in free variation. It is also the case that a devoiced velar plosive [g̊] occurs word-finally; so that we could hypothesize that [d̥] and [g̊] were in free variation. But we soon realize that the substitution of one for the other makes a difference in the word: *bid* [bɪd̥] and *big* [bɪg̊] are different words.

Phonetic similarity

These two criteria—complementary distribution and free variation—by themselves leave a loophole, which has to be filled by the criterion of **phonetic similarity**. In English, on the basis of the criterion of complementary distribution, the voiceless glottal fricative (h) and the voiced velar nasal (ŋ) would be members of the same phoneme, since [h] occurs only word-initially and [ŋ] occurs only word-medially and word-finally. But, quite obviously, it is ridiculous to suppose that these two sounds have anything in common: a glance at their descriptive labels reveals that they share nothing—not in terms of voicing, nor place of articulation, nor manner of articulation. This insight is formalized in the criterion of phonetic similarity, which states that if two or more phones are to be members of the same phoneme they must be phonetically similar. In practice, this means that the allophones of a phoneme usually share at least two of voicing, place of articulation and manner of articulation in common.

English phonemes and allophones

A phoneme may be defined, then, as a class of phonetically similar phones in complementary distribution or in free variation or in both. Remembering that a transcription in terms of phones is a narrow transcription and is enclosed in square brackets, and a transcription in terms of phonemes is a broad transcription and is enclosed in slashed brackets, we shall now turn to a detailed consideration of English sounds (phonemes) and their variants (allophones).

Plosives

We begin with plosive sounds, which as a class show more variation than any other. We have already noted, in Chapter 2, that voiceless plosives in English (p, t, k) may be either aspirated (accompanied by a puff of air on release) or unaspirated. That is to say, the phonemes /p/, /t/ and /k/ each have an aspirated allophone [pʰ], [tʰ] and [kʰ], and an unaspirated allophone [p], [t] and [k]. And these allophones are in complementary distribution: the unaspirated allophone occurs after /s/ and the aspirated allophone occurs in all other positions. As we pointed out in Chapter 2, though, the degree of aspiration varies from environment to environment. There is strong aspiration when the plosive occurs initially in a stressed syllable eg in *pin, tin, kin*. Between vowels the aspiration tends to be rather weak, and may indeed be absent altogether eg in *upper, utter, sucker*: we could say that we have a case of allophones in free variation in this instance. And in final position the amount of aspiration is variable, depending whether the plosive is released fully or not eg as in *sip, sit, sick*.

The voiced plosives in English /b, d, g/ may be considered to have two allophones. The main allophone, and the one which occurs in all environments, is the fully voiced [b], [d], [g]. The other allophone occurs only in word-final position and is a devoiced variant [b̥], [d̥], [g̥]. It is in free variation with the fully voiced allophone, that is, either of them may occur in this position with no particular factor conditioning the occurrence of one rather than the other, except for the speaker's whim at the time eg as in *rib, rid, rig*.

The difference between /p, t, k/ and /b, d, g/ in English is not merely one of voicing, or even unequivocally one of voicing; that is, the distinction between voiced and voiceless. It is also a difference of aspiration. The one environment in which unaspirated voiceless plosives regularly occur, ie after /s/, is the one in which voiced plosives do not occur: there are no English words beginning with /sb/, /sd/ or /sg/. There is, therefore, no contrast between voiceless and voiced plosives in English in this environment. In all other environments (initially, finally, intervocalically) /p, t, k/ and /b, d, g/ are distinguished both by voicing and usually also by aspiration. In fact, aspiration might be said to be more important in distinguishing /p, t, k/ (or words containing them) from /b, d, g/ (or words containing them), cf *pip/bib, tit/did, kick/gig.*

For this and other reasons, the series /p, t, k/ are often referred to not as 'voiceless' plosives, but as **fortis** plosives; and the /b, d, g/ series not as 'voiced plosives, but as **lenis** plosives. The terms fortis and lenis refer to the muscular energy used in articulation: fortis consonants are more energetically articulated than lenis consonants. These terms are used not only for plosives, but also for fricatives and affricates in English.

The variants of plosive that we have dealt with so far involve the whole class of plosives in English. We now consider variants of individual members of the class. Besides the allophones already mentioned, the alveolar plosives each have a further allophone. In words like *width* /wɪdθ/ and *eighth* /eɪtθ/ the articulation of the plosive is not alveolar, but dental: the tongue tip makes a closure with the back of the upper front teeth, rather than with the alveolar ridge. In other words, the articulation of the plosive is the same here as that of the following dental fricative, and this allophone occurs only in this environment. So /d/ has an allophone [d̪] before a dental fricative, and /t/ has an allophone [t̪] before a dental fricative.

Velar plosives also have variants in addition to those already mentioned. Compare the articulation of the velar plosives in the following words: *keep/geese, cup/gum, coop/goose.* By careful observation you will feel that the contact of the tongue with the roof of the mouth is made in a slightly different position for each of the three pairs of words. The closure of the velar in the first pair is more forward than that of the second pair, and the closure of the velar in the last pair is further back than that in the middle pair. The conditioning factor is the nature of the vowel that follows the initial velar plosive: a front vowel, as in *keep*/kip/ or *geese* /gis/ tends to pull the articulation forward, and a back vowel, as in *coop* /kup/ and *goose* /gus/, tends to push the articulation back. So if we regard the articulation of the velar before central vowels, as in *cup* /kʌp/ and *gum* /gʌm/, as genuinely velar, we can call the articulation before front vowels 'pre-velar' and the articulation before back vowels 'post-velar'. So the phoneme /k/ has an allophone [k̟] or [k̟ʰ] before front vowels, and an allophone [k̠] or [k̠ʰ] before back vowels; and the phoneme /g/ has an allophone [g̟] before front vowels and an allophone [g̠] before back vowels.

One further variant needs to be mentioned for plosives. When a voiceless (or fortis) alveolar plosive /t/ occurs in final position in a syllable, it may be articulated as a glottal stop eg in *suit.* So the phoneme /t/ has allophone [ʔ] occuring in syllable final position, and which is in free variation with [tʰ].

Laterals

We have already mentioned the fact that the alveolar lateral /l/ in English has two allophones, a non-velarized allophone [l], occurring before vowels and /j/, as in *leave, early, illuminate,* and a velarized allophone [ɫ], occurring before consonants, /w/ and word-finally (ie before pause), as in *altogether, always, pool.* These allophones are, then, in complementary distribution. There is, in addition, a third allophone which is in complementary distribution with these two: after a fortis (ie voiceless) plosive /p, k/ the alveolar lateral in English is devoiced (ie voiceless), eg in *play, clean.* So the phoneme /l/ has the allophone [l̥] after /p, k/. There is yet one more allophone of /l/ in complementary distribution with the others: like the alveolar plosives, the alveolar lateral has a dental articulation when it occurs immediately before a dental fricative, as in *filth, stealth, although.* Since this occurrence is before a consonant, the allophone is also velarized: [l̴].

'r' sounds

In (Chapter 2) we said that a number of 'r'-sounds occur in English speech. It is possible to recognize three regularly occurring allophones of the /r/ phoneme in English. The allophone with the widest distribution is the post-alveolar frictionless continuant [ɹ]. After fortis consonants /p, t, k, f, θ, ʃ etc/ a devoiced (voiceless) allophone occurs [ɹ̥] eg in *train, crane, free, shrug.* These two allophones are in complementary distribution. The third possible allophone is a flapped consonant [ɾ], which may occur intervocalically eg in *very, marry.* This allophone is in free variation with the voiced post-alveolar frictionless continuant. While other 'r'-sounds do occur in the speech of English native speakers eg a rolled consonant /r/ or a uvular roll /R/, they do not occur regularly enough for them to be included in a general description of English sounds.

Nasals

Among the nasals we have to consider two variants. Like its alveolar counterparts among the plosives and laterals, the alveolar nasal has a dental articulation before dental fricatives as in *plinth, ninth.* So the phoneme /n/ has an allophone [n̪] occurring before dentals, and an allophone [n] occurring elsewhere; they are in complementary distribution. The other variant occurs as an allophone of both the bilabial nasal and the aveolar nasal. When these occur before a labio-dental fricative /f, v/ as in *symphony, convent* they are often articulated as a labio-dental nasal [ɱ]. This allophone is probably in free variation with the normal allophone [m] and [n]; its occurrence is more likely, the more rapidly a person speaks. So the phoneme /m/ has an allophone [ɱ] before labio-dental fricatives, which is in free variation with the normal allophone [m]; and the phoneme /n/ has an allophone [ɱ] before labio-dental fricatives, which is in free variation with the normal allophone [n].

Fricatives

Lastly among the consonants we come to the fricatives. Like voiced plosives, voiced fricatives have a devoiced allophone occurring word-finally (before a pause), which is in free variation with the normal fully voiced allophone eg *rise* [z̥], *live* [v̥], *seethe* [ð̥]. The palato-alveolar fricatives /ʃ, ʒ/ present at an interesting case for the application of phoneme theory to English. They could almost be regarded as allophones of the same phoneme. The voiced palato-alveolar fricative /ʒ/ occurs only intervocalically, except for a few loan-words from French, where it may occur initially and finally; although, as pointed out earlier, many speakers substitute a palato-alveolar affricate in these positions. Moreover, there is hardly a pair of words in which /ʃ/ and /ʒ/ contrast; the nearest is perhaps *fission* and *vision*. However, the fact that /ʃ/ does occur intervocalically eg also in *mission, cushion, bushel,* means that the two sounds cannot be considered to be in complementary distribution or in free variation, and so must be separate phonemes.

Vowels

The English vowels can be divided into two groups: a number of the pure vowels and all the diphthongs are in general longer in duration than the remainder of the pure vowels. A comparison of *seat* and *sit* will make it plain that the vowel of *seat* /i/ has a longer duration than the vowel of *sit* /ɪ/. The set of short vowels is /ɪ, ɛ, æ, ʌ, ɒ, ʊ, ə/ and the set of long vowels /iː, uː, ɑː, ɔː, ɜː/ together with the diphthongs. The symbol : denotes length. Some of these vowels may be matched into pairs of complementary long and short vowels eg /iː, ɪ/, /uː, ʊ/, /ɑː, æ/, /ɔː, ɒ/, /ɜː, ə/ but it is important to note that the distinguishing factor between these vowels is primarily one of quality determined by difference of articulation, and not one of length.

The short vowels have no variants. The long vowels and diphthongs, however, vary in length according to the environment in which they occur. They can be considered to have two allophones: (1) a short allophone before a fortis consonant ie /p, t, k, tʃ, f, θ, s, ʃ/; (2) a long allophone in all other environments. Compare, for example, the length of the vowels in *bead/beat, rude/root, card/cart, cause/course, curd/curt.* The long allophone may be marked with a length mark eg [iː] and the short allophone without eg [i]. In broad (phonemic) transcription, there will be no need to indicate the length of long vowels at all, since it is not a phonemically distinguishing characteristic. But in a narrow (phonetic) transcription the long vowels will need to be marked for length when they occur in environments where they are relatively long, ie not before fortis consonants.

Neutralization

One further topic remains to be dealt with under the heading of sounds and their variants: **neutralization**. We have referred to phonemes as contrastive units of sound: the substitution of one phoneme for another will result in a different word being formed, cf *pin/bin/tin/sin/thin, bit/bet/bat/boot/bait/boat/but/bite/bought/beat* etc. Sometimes, however, in a particular environment, the contrast between phonemes in a particular set will be neutralized: the normal contrast will not operate. We have already mentioned an instance of this in English, though without using the term 'neutralization'. This was the neutralization of the contrast between fortis (voiceless) and lenis (voiced) plosives after /s/. The plosive after /s/ is unaspirated and voiceless: the first feature it shares with /b, d, g/ the second with /p, t, k/. The contrast between /p, t, k/ and /b, d, g/ is neutralized in this environment, since there are no words in English that differ from each other by the fact that one begins with /sp/ and the other with /sb/ (or /st/, /sd/ and /sk/, /sg/). In fact, the phone occurring in this environment could be considered an allophone of either the fortis set or the lenis set. It is usually allocated to the fortis set, however, and this is reflected in the orthography.

Another case of neutralization occurs in English among the nasals /m, n, ŋ/ when they occur before fortis plosives /p, t, k/. This is a slightly different case from the preceding one. Here the neutralization of contrast between /m/, /n/ and /ŋ/ arises from the fact that which of these nasals occurs is totally predictable from the following plosive: a bilabial nasal occurs only before a bilabial plosive, an alveolar nasal before an alveolar plosive, and a velar nasal only before a velar plosive, as in *limp, lint, link*. That is to say, only the combinations /mp/, /nt/ and /ŋk/ occur, and not the combinations /mt/, /mk/, /np/, /nk/, /ŋp/, /ŋt/.

From what has been said in this chapter it will be clear that the list of the 44 sounds of English at the end of Chapter 3 represents an inventory of the phonemes of English, those units which arc regarded as being contrastive, making a difference in words if one is substituted for another. By way of summary for this chapter, there now follows the same list, together with the allophones of each phoneme:

Consonants

/p/	[p] after /s/, [pʰ] elsewhere
/b/	[b̥] word-finally (free variation), [b] normally
/t/	[t] after /s/, [t̪ʰ] before /θ, ð/, [ʔ] word-finally (free variation) [tʰ] elsewhere
/d/	[d̪] before /θ, ð/, [d̥] word-finally (free variation), [d] elsewhere
/k/	[k̟ʰ] before front vowels, [k̠ʰ] before back vowels, [k] after /s/, [kʰ] elsewhere
/g/	[g̟] before front vowels, [ḡ] before back vowels, [g̥] word-finally (free variation), [g] elsewhere
/f/	[f]
/v/	[v̥] word-finally (free variation), [v] normally
/θ/	[θ]
/ð/	[ð̥] word-finally (free variation), [ð] normally
/s/	[s]
/z/	[z̥] word-finally (free variation), [z] normally
/ʃ/	[ʃ]
/ʒ/	[ʒ]
/h/	[h]
/m/	[ɱ] before /f, v/ (free variation), [m̩] elsewhere
/n/	[n̪] before /θ, ð/, [ɱ] before /f, v/ (free variation), [n] elsewhere
/ŋ/	[ŋ]
/l/	[l̥] after /p, k/, [ɫ̪] before /θ, ð/, [ɫ] before consonant, pause, [l] elsewhere
/r/	[ɹ̥] after fortis consonant, [ɾ] intervocalically (free variation) [ɹ] elsewhere
/w/	[w]
/j/	[j]

Vowels

/i/	[i] before fortis consonant, [i:] elsewhere

/ɪ/   [ɪ]
/ɛ/   [ɛ]
/æ/   [æ]
/ɑ/   [ɑ] before fortis consonant, [ɑ:] elsewhere
/ɒ/   [ɒ]
/ɔ/   [ɔ] before fortis consonant, [ɔ:] elsewhere
/ʊ/   [ʊ]
/u/   [u] before fortis consonant, [u:] elsewhere
/ə/   [ə]
/ɜ/   [ɜ] before fortis consonant, [ɜ:] elsewhere
/ʌ/   [ʌ]
/eɪ/   [eɪ] before fortis consonant, [eɪ:] elsewhere
/aɪ/   [aɪ] before fortis consonant, [aɪ:] elsewhere
/ɒɪ/   [ɒɪ] before fortis consonant, [ɒɪ:] elsewhere
/əʊ/   [əʊ] before fortis consonant, [əʊ:] elsewhere
/aʊ/   [aʊ] before fortis consonant, [aʊ:] elsewhere
/ɪə/   [ɪə] before fortis consonant, [ɪə:] elsewhere
/ɛə/   [ɛə] before fortis consonant, [ɛə:] elsewhere
/ʊə/   [ʊə] before fortis consonant, [ʊə:] elsewhere.

Exercise 5

Make a broad (phonemic) and a narrow (phonetic) transcription of the following English words.
eg *breadth* /brɛdθ/ [bɹɛd̪θ], *purple* /pɜpəl/ [pʰɜpʰəɫ], *shaving-stick* /ʃeɪvɪŋstɪk/ [ʃeɪ ːvɪŋstɪkʰ]

1. freak	2. wealth	3. kettle
4. plinth	5. Thursday	6. achieve
7. gorgeous	8. comfortable	9. percussion
10. writhe	11. alcohol	12. thirsty
13. reject	14. probe	15. especially
16. mild	17. caustic	18. paramount
19. conversion	20. pleasing	21. favourite
22. receive	23. unsure	24. ablaze
25. screech		

5. Sounds in connected speech

All the variations in pronunciation that we considered in the previous chapter were in the pronunciation of words as units in isolation. Changes such as /n/ to [n̪] before /θ/ we accounted for by word-internal factors, or by the assumption of pause at the end of the word, as for example in the conditions for the occurrence of a velarized alveolar lateral [ɫ]. But we rarely speak in single word utterances. And in studying the phonetics of a language we have to take account of the kinds of changes in pronunciation that take place as a result of words being strung together. Most of these changes occur at word boundaries and affect the final and initial sounds of words.

Assimilation

Some of the allophonic variation which occurs within words, that we discussed in the previous chapter, occurs also at word boundaries. Alveolar consonants at the end of a word have a dental articulation if the initial sound of the following word is a dental fricative eg the dental allophone [t̪] of /t/ occurs in *not thin* [nɒt̪ θɪn]. Here there is in fact no aspiration of the alveolar plosive, because it is unreleased, the release occurring through the following fricative. In *ten thumps*, the dental allophone [n̪] of /n/ occurs: [tʰɛn̪ θʌmpʰs]. And in *well thought*, the dental allophone [ɫ̪] of /l/ occurs: [wɛɫ̪ θɔtʰ]. A second case of allophonic variation occurring at a word boundary is the substitution of a labio-dental nasal for a bilabial or alveolar nasal before a labio-dental fricative. In the sequence *ten forks*, the alveolar nasal may have the labio-dental variant [ɱ] in a fairly rapid pronunciation; and in the sequence *come for me* the bilabial nasal at the end of *come* may have the labio-dental variant in a rapid delivery. A third case of allophonic variation occurring at word boundaries as well as within words is the incidence of the voiceless (devoiced) allophones of /l/ and /r/ ie [l̥] and [ɹ̥], when these phonemes occur after a fortis (voiceless) consonant. So in the sequence *at last*, the initial alveolar lateral of *last* is devoiced after the fortis alveolar plosive: [ətʰl̥ɑst]. And in the sequence *at rest*, the post-alveolar frictionless continuant is likewise devoiced: [ətʰ ɹ̥ɛst].

There is a further case of variation at word boundaries which could be considered as allophonic variation, but this is not a kind which occurs within words. This is the case of word-final labio-dental fricatives having a bilabial articulation when the initial sound of the following word is a bilabial plosive. This probably only occurs in a fairly rapid delivery. For example, in the sequence *rough patch*, the final labio-dental fricative of *rough* may become [Φ] in rapid pronunciation: [rʌΦ pʰætʃ]. And in the sequence *live bird*, the final voiced labio-dental fricative of *live* may become [β] in rapid pronunciation: [laɪːβ bɜːd].

The conditions that we gave for the occurrence of one allophone of a phoneme rather than another applied to words spoken in isolation. It happens in a couple of cases that these conditions no longer apply in a sequence of words, particularly in relation to word-final position. One of the conditions for the occurrence of a velarized alveolar lateral is word-final position; but if an alveolar lateral word-finally is followed by a vowel in initial position in the subsequent word, then it is non-velarized eg in the sequence *fill it* compared with *fill*: [fɪl ɪtʰ], [fɪɫ]. We said that lenis (voiced) plosives and fricatives tend to be devoiced in word-final position. But if, in a sequence, the word following begins with a vowel or voiced consonant, then they will not be devoiced, though they will be if the initial sound of the following word is a voiceless consonant. Compare *good dates* [gʊd deɪtʰs] with *good trees* [gʊd̥ tʰɫ̥iːz].

The influence of one sound on another to become more like itself is called **assimilation**. Assimilation may be to the place of articulation of a neighbouring sound, as in the dentalization of alveolars before dental fricatives, or the substitution of a labio-dental nasal for a bilabial or alveolar nasal before a labio-dental fricative. Or assimilation may be in voicing, as when voiced plosives and fricatives become devoiced before voiceless sounds or silence (pause), or when /l/ and /r/ become voiceless after fortis (voiceless) consonants.

All the cases of assimilation that we have considered so far have been cases of allophonic variation: the substitutions have been regarded as allophones of the same phoneme, with the criterion of phonetic similarity being of particular relevance here eg in counting [ɸ] and [β] as allophones of /f/ and /v/ respectively. But there are many cases of assimilation where the substitution is not allophonic but phonemic, the substitution of one phoneme for another.

Alveolar sounds in word-final position are particularly liable to assimilate to the place of articulation of the initial consonant of a following word; that is, the sounds /t, d, n, s, z/. Final /t/ is likely to become /p/ before bilabial sounds /p, b, m/ eg in the sequences *that pen* [ðæp pʰɛn], *that boy* [ðæp bɒɪ], *that man* [ðæp mæn]. And final /d/ becomes /b/ before the same sounds eg in *good pen* [gʊb pʰɛn] etc. Final /t/ is likely to become /k/ before velar plosives /k, g/ eg in the sequences *that cup* [ðæk kʰʌ pʰ], *that girl* [ðæk gɜ ːɫ]. And likewise /d/ becomes /g/ before the same sounds eg in *good cup* [gʊg kʰʌpʰ] etc.

A word-final alveolar nasal /n/ becomes bilabial /m/ before bilabial sounds /p, b, m/ and velar /ŋ/ before velar plosives /k, g/. Examples: *ten pens* [tʰɛm pʰɛnz], *ten boys* [tʰɛm bɒɪ ːz], *ten men* [tʰɛm mɛn]; *ten cups* [tʰɛŋ kʰʌpʰs], *ten girls* [tʰɛŋ gɜ ːɫz]. If a sequence of alveolar nasal and alveolar plosive occurs word-finally, then both may assimilate to the place of articulation of a following consonant. Examples: /nt/ in *don't* assimilates to the place of articulation of the following /b/ in *don't be late* [dəʊ ː mp bɪ leɪtʰ]; /nt/ in *won't* assimilates to /k/ in *he won't come* [hɪ wəʊ ːŋ k kʰʌ m]; /nd/ in *found* assimilates to the bilabial articulation of following /b/ in *he found both* [hɪ faʊ ːmb bəʊθ]; /nd/ in *kind* assimilates to the velar articulation of /g/ in *a kind gift* [ə kʰaɪ ːŋg g̊ɪftʰ].

Alveolar fricatives /s, z/ assimilate to a following palatal sound, either palato-alveolar fricative or palatal frictionless continuant /ʃ, j/ and become palato-alveolar fricatives /ʃ, ʒ/. Examples: *this shop* [ðɪʃ ʃɒpʰ], *this year* [ðɪʃ jɪə ː]; *has she* [hæʒ ʃi ː], *those young men* [ðəʊ ːʒ jʌŋ mɛn].

Assimilations of the kind we have been discussing could, in theory, give rise to ambiguous utterances, since in substituting one phoneme for another the new phoneme may already make an acceptable sequence in English. For example, the sequence [ɹæŋkʰwɪkʰli] could be taken as representing either *rang quickly* or *ran quickly* with assimilation of /n/ to following /k/. Or the sequence [wɒtʃ jɔ ː weɪtʰ] could represent either *watch your weight* or *what's your weight* with assimilation of /s/ to following palatal /j/.

When word-final alveolar plosives and fricatives /t, d, s, z/ are followed by an initial palatal frictionless continuant /j/, then assimilation is to palato-alveolar place of articulation and the initial /j/ usually disappears, although for /s, z/ this is not always the case, as indicated above. The alveolar plosives become palato-alveolar affricates /tʃ, dʒ/ in this instance, and the alveolar fricatives become palato-alveolar fricatives /ʃ, ʒ/, as discussed earlier. Examples: *would you* [wʊdʒ uː], *what you want* [wɒtʃ uː wɒntʰ]; *as yet* [æʒɛtʰ], *in case you need it* [ɪŋ kʰeɪʃuː niːd ɪtʰ].

Now we come to assimilations involving nasalization. A voiced alveolar plosive /d/ may become a nasal when followed by a nasal. If the following nasal is alveolar, /d/ becomes /n/, eg in the sequence *he wouldn't do it*, the /d/ of *would* becomes an alveolar nasal: [hɪ wʊnn(t) duː ɪtʰ]. There is a tendency for the /t/ of *not* to disappear. If the following nasal is velar, then /d/ becomes /ŋ/; eg in the sequence *he wouldn't go*, the /nt/ assimilate to the following velar /g/, and the /d/ of *would* then assimilates to the velar nasal following, while the /k/ from /t/ probably disappears: [hɪ wʊŋŋ(k) gəʊ ː]. If the following nasal is bilabial, then /d/ becomes /m/, assimilating again both in place of articulation and in nasality eg *good morning* [gʊm mɔ ːnɪŋ]. It is not just word-final alveolar consonants that may be involved in assimilation; for example, the voiced labio-dental fricative /v/ may assimilate in place and nasality to a following bilabial nasal /m/, as in *you can have mine* [ju kŋ hæm maɪ ːn]. In this sequence also the vowel of *can* probably disappears (see further below on reduction) and the final alveolar nasal /n/ assimilates towards the glottal articulation of /h/ and becomes velar.

Finally we turn to assimilations involving voice. Word-final lenis (voiced) fricatives may become fortis (voiceless) when they are followed by an initial fortis consonant, especially if the two words are part of a closely knit group. Examples: /ð/ becomes /θ/ in *with thanks* [wɪθ θæŋkʰs], *breathe slowly* [bɹiːθ sləʊ ːlɪ]; /z/ becomes /s/ in *these socks* [ðis sɒkʰs], *he was sent* [hɪ wəs sɛntʰ]; /v/ becomes /f/ in *of course* [ɒf kʰɔs], *we've found it* [wif faʊ ːnd ɪtʰ]; /dʒ/ becomes [tʃ] in *bridge score* [bɹɪtʃ skɔ ː].

Assimilation is a widespread phenomenon in speech. The instances that we have discussed represent the main ones in English. Quite obviously they do not necessarily occur all the time; but a statement about assimilation implies that when people speak, and the more rapidly they do so, then these kinds of alteration may take place. Since this is so, these variations will need to be taken account of in a narrow transcription of speech. Indeed, it may be argued that the phonemic variation resulting from assimilation should even be accounted for in a broad transcription. But for practical purposes we shall assume that a broad transcription represents words as if spoken in isolation.

By way of further illustration, here is an imagined short conversation between a policeman and a motorist in narrow transcription including assimilations (underlined).

—*Good morning, sir.*   [g̃ʊm̱ mɔːnɪŋ sɜː
—*Good morning, officer.*   g̃ʊm̱ mɔːnɪŋ ɒfɪsə
—*Your stop light's not working*   jɔ stɒpʰ ḻaɪtʰs nɒp̱ wɜkʰɪŋ
—*It was when I left the house.*   ɪp̱ wɒz wɛn aɪː lɛ ̱f̱ṯ ðə haʊs
—*That's not quite now.*   ðætʰs nɒḵ kʰwaɪt naʊː
—*Which one might it be?*   wɪtʃ wʌm̱ maɪtʰ ɪp̱ biː
—*The left light.*   ðə ˈlɛftʰ ḻaɪtʰ
—*I'll have to get the thing fixed.*   aɪː ɫ hæf̱ tʰə gɛṯ ðə θɪŋ fɪkʰst]

Exercise 6

Make a narrow transcription of the following sequences of words, including any possible assimilations.
eg *Shut the yard gate behind you* [ʃʌṯ ðə jɑːg geɪp bɪhaɪːndʒuː]

1. They train cows to jump
2. A bad picture of a rose tree
3. Who do you want?
4. He was shipwrecked
5. He's found seven fake pictures.

Elision

Besides assimilation, there are two further processes that cause variation in the pronunciation of sounds at word boundaries: **elision** and **liaison**. The process of elision involves the complete disappearance of a sound and takes place only in fairly rapid speech. In such speech it is very common for word-initial /h/ to disappear—and this is a characteristic by no means restricted to cockney speakers! Example: *up the hill* [ʌpʰ ðɪ ɪɫ].

In word-final position it is the alveolar plosives that are most likely to undergo the process of elision, particularly if they are preceded by another consonant and the following word has a consonant in initial position. The pairs of word-final consonants for which this is the case can be divided into two groups. The first of these comprises continuant consonants followed by /t/ or /d/: /st, ft, ʃt, nd, ld, zd, ðd, vd/. Examples: *next day* [nɛkʰs deɪː], *left turn* [lɛf tʰɜːn], *mashed potatoes* [mæʃ pʰətheɪtʰəʊːz], *bend back* [bɛm bækʰ], *hold tight* [həʊːɫ tʰaɪtʰ], *refused both* [ɹɪfjuːz bəʊθ], *loathed beer* [ləʊːð bɪəː], *moved back* [muːv bækʰ]. The second group comprises plosives and affricates followed by /t/ or /d/: /pt, kt, tʃt, bd, gd, dʒd/. Examples: *kept quiet* [kʰɛpʰ kʰwaɪːətʰ], *liked jam* [laɪkʰ dʒæm], *reached Paris* [ɹiːtʃ pʰælɪs], *robbed both* [ɹɒb bəʊθ], *lagged behind* [læg bɪhaɪːnd], *changed colour* [tʃeɪːndʒ kʰʌlə].

Word-final /t/ may undergo elision in two further circumstances. If the initial sound of the following word is /t/ or /d/, then the resulting cluster of /tt/ or /td/ is often simplified to /t/ or /d/ respectively. Examples: *I've got to go* [aɪ ːv gɒ tʰə gəʊ ː], *what do you want* [wɒ dʒu ː wɒntʰ]. The second case involves the negator *not* when it is reduced to /nt/, and the /t/ undergoes elision before another consonant. Examples: *you mustn't lose it* [ju mʌsn luːz ɪtʰ], *doesn't she know* [dʌzn ʃiːnəʊ ː]. This is similar to the continuant +/t, d/ cases discussed above.

Liaison

Liaison, the other process occurring at word boundaries, involves the insertion of a sound that is by and large unmotivated from the phonetic context. The sound is /r/. And it is by and large unmotivated, because, although an /r/ occurs in the written form of some of the words involved, reflecting an earlier pronunciation, the use of linking /r/ has been extended to contexts where there is no *r* in thc orthographic form. In thc sequences *here and there* [ɪəɹ ən ðɛə], *father and son* [fɑ ːðə ɹ ən sʌn], and *the far east* [ðə fɑ ː ɹ ist] an *r* occurs in the written form, although not if the words concerned are pronounced in isolation: [hɪə], [fɑ ːðə], [fɑ ː]. But in the sequences *law and order* [lɔ ː ɹ ən ɔ ːdə] and *the idea of it* [ðɪ aɪ ːdɪə ː ɹ əv ɪtʰ] there is no *r* in the orthography and yet liaison takes place.

Reduction

There is one further process that occurs as the result of rapidly articulated speech, but it is not one that occurs at word boundaries. It is called **reduction** and involves the substitution of a 'weak' central vowel, especially /ə/ or /ɪ/, for a peripheral vowel ie front or back. Reduction occurs particularly in unstressed syllables of words with more than one syllable, and in single syllable words that have a grammatical (rather than a lexical) function, eg words like *is, are, have, of, his, the, does, and, a, an.* (Syllables are discussed in Chapter 6 and the distinction between grammatical and lexical words in Chapter 9.)

It is impossible to give a detailed list of all the possible reductions, but the following examples will provide a fair idea of the kinds of cases that may occur. Take the word *of*, pronounced in isolation as /ɒv/. In connected speech this would commonly be pronounced [əv], and may even be reduced further to [v] or [ə] eg in *two of mine* [tuː ə(v) maɪ ːn]. In isolation *have* would be pronounced /hæv/, but in connected speech the /h/ will undergo elision and the front vowel /æ/ will be reduced, giving [əv], eg in *they have eaten* [ðeɪ ː əv iʰtʰən]. The word *the*, pronounced in isolation as /ðiː/, may in connected speech be either [ðɪ], if it occurs before a word beginning with a vowel, or [ðə] before an initial consonant. In isolation *and* is pronounced /ænd/, but in connected speech as [ənd], or more frequently as [ən] or even [n].

In unstressed syllables that end in /l/ or /n/ the vowel is normally the unstressed mid central spread vowel /ə/ eg in *bottle* /bɒtʰəl/ or *button* /bʌtʰən/. But in connected speech a further reduction often occurs which causes the vowel to be dropped completely, giving [bɒtʰɫ̩] and [bʌtʰn̩]. Normally a syllable has to contain a vowel (see Chapter 6), but in this case the /l/ and /n/ are doing service for the vowel and are called syllabic /l/ and syllabic /n/ respectively. The symbol for a syllabic consonant is the small stroke beneath the consonant symbol: [l̩], [n̩].

As in the case of assimilation, a narrow transcription of a connected sequence of speech will have to take account of the processes of elision, liaison and reduction. By way of summary, here is a list of the processes described in this chapter that occur when words are put together in connected speech.

Assimilation

Word-final alveolars become dental before dental fricatives.
Bilabial and alveolar nasals become labio-dental before labio-dental fricatives.
Word-initial /l/ and /r/ becomes voiceless after fortis consonants.
Word-final labio-dental fricatives may become bilabial before bilabial plosives.
Word-final /l/ is non-velarised if followed by an initial vowel.
Word-final lenis plosives and fricatives are not devoiced if followed by a vowel or voiced consonant.
Word-final /t, d/ become bilabial before bilabial consonants.
Word-final /t, d/ become velar before velar plosives.
Word-final /n/ becomes bilabial before bilabial consonants.
Word-final /n/ becomes velar before velar plosives.
Word-final /nt, nd/ both become bilabial before bilabials and velar before velars.
Word-final /s, z/ become palato-alveolar before palato-alveolar fricatives and the palatal frictionless continuant.
Word-final /t, d, s, z/ become palato-alveolar affricates (/t, d/) or fricatives (/s, z/) before /j/ and /j/ disappears.
Word-final /d/ becomes a nasal before a nasal, at the place of articulation of the nasal.
Word-final /v/ becomes a nasal before a nasal.
Word-final lenis fricatives become fortis before an initial fortis consonant.

Elision

Word-initial /h/ frequently undergoes elision.
Word-final /t, d/ preceded by another consonant and followed by an initial consonant undergo elision.
Word-final /t/ followed by /t, d/ undergoes elision.

Liaison

Word-final vowel followed by an initial vowel are often linked by insertion of /r/.

Reduction

Vowels in unstressed syllables, or in monosyllabic grammatical words are often reduced to /ɪ/ or /ə/.
Complete reduction, ie elision, may occur in unstressed syllables ending in /l/ or /n/, giving a syllabic consonant.

Exercise 7

Make a narrow transcription of the following utterances, taking account of any assimilation, elision, liaison and reduction.

eg *He stole the soft fruit off that greengrocer*

[ɪ stəʊːɬ ð̩ə sɒf frutʰ ɒf ð̩æk griːŋɡləʊsə]

1. What did you say his name was?
2. We discussed the idea of Ivan's last Tuesday.
3. He didn't come to the lecture or he would have known.
4. They camped by the river on the other side.
5. The masked gunman held the hostage at gunpoint.

6. Combining sounds

Phonemes themselves have no meaning: their only function is to combine together to form higher-level meaningful units; that is, words. But between phonemes and words we have to recognize an intermediate level of phonological organization: the **syllable**. Many words in English have only one syllable; they are 'monosyllabic'. But many have more than one syllable; they are 'polysyllabic'. And yet it is clear that the same principles operate in the combining of phonemes into syllables, whether the syllable itself constitutes a word, or whether the syllable in turn combines with another or several other syllables to form a word. Like phonemes, syllables are in principle meaningless eg *sim* /sɪm/ and *ple* /pəl/ of *simple*, even though in some cases they do coincide with a meaningful unit, eg in *hard—ship, un—do* or, of course, in monosyllabic words.

Syllabic structure

A syllable has a basic three-part structure, composed of a central part and a peripheral part before and after the central one. The central part is almost always a vowel sound and the peripheral parts are consonants. Each syllable has only one vowel, either a pure vowel or a dipthong, at its centre; but the number of consonants in the peripheries may vary. It is possible that one or other or both of the peripheral parts will not be realised ie there may be no consonants either before or after the vowel, as for example in *out* /aʊt/, *toe* /təʊ/, *I* /aɪ/. In English there may, in fact, be up to three consonants before the vowel and up to four consonants after it eg in *strengths* /strɛŋkθs/. Phonemes, then, combine to form syllables, and syllables combine to form words. The maximum number of syllables possible in an English word seems to be about seven or eight eg in *in—ter—natio—na—li—za—tion.*

We have said that a vowel is almost always at the central part of a syllable. The exceptions to this statement are the so-called syllabic consonants, discussed in Chapter 5, which arise from the reduction of a weak vowel to extinction. The consonants which most often become central in the syllable for this reason are /l/ and /n/, as in the examples given in Chapter 5: *bottle* /bɒtl̩/, *button* /bʌtn̩/. In some other languages syllabic consonants are normal central elements, eg a form of *r* in Czech. Vowels in English never function at the peripheries of syllables, and this provides the reason for treating the 'semi-vowels' /w/ and /j/ as consonants: in spite of their vowel-like quality they pattern in syllable structure like consonants, ie they occur in the peripheries of syllables and not in the central part.

One practical reason for recognizing syllables as intermediate units between phonemes and words is that they represent the most convenient level at which to describe the way in which phonemes combine together and the restrictions that occur on combinations of phonemes. The possibilities of phoneme combination are not unlimited: any phoneme may not combine with just any other. There is the obvious restriction imposed by the nature of syllable structure Consonant-Vowel-Consonant (CVC); a syllable could not be composed of just consonants, nor of more than one vowel or diphthong. But even taking this restriction into account, some phoneme combinations would be impossible to pronounce eg /pgnusr/, except perhaps with extreme difficulty. Other combinations, although in principle quite pronounceable, just do not occur in English, eg /ŋɪfk/. English does not use all the possible pronounceable combinations of phonemes to make syllables and words. That is to say, there are certain rules of phoneme combination for English which can be deduced from the syllables and words actually occurring.

Initial periphery

Since the nature of the syllable itself specifies that only one vowel phoneme may occur in each syllable, we can describe the rules of phoneme combination in terms of the consonants and their combinations that may occur in peripheral positions in syllables. We shall look first at the consonants in initial position in the syllable. It is possible that no consonant at all will occur before the vowel (as in *out*), and that is the case in English before all the vowel phonemes except two: /ʊ/ and /ʊə/ never occur without a consonant preceding. All the consonant phonemes of English may occur singly in syllable initial position except two: /ʒ/ and /ŋ/ never occur by themselves, nor for that matter in combination with another consonant, in the initial periphery of an English syllable. The permissible combinations of two consonants in syllable initial position may be expressed by the following diagram:

Figure 25: Syllable-initial two-consonant combinations

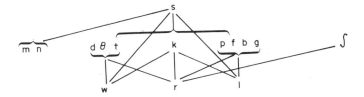

According to this diagram the following syllable initial two consonant combinations are possible: /sm/, /sn/, /st/, /sk/, /sp/, /sf/, /dw/, θw/, /tw/, /dr/, /θr/, /tr/, /kw/, /kr/, /kl/, /pr/, /fr/, /br/, /gr/, /pl/, /fl/, /bl/, /gl/, /ʃr/, /sw/, /sl/, making a total of 26. This obviously represents only a very small proportion of the arithmetically possible combinations of the 24 consonants in English, which would amount to 576, assuming that each consonant would be allowed to occur with itself. The restrictions are even more remarkable when we turn to combinations of three consonants in syllable initial position. Here the arithmetical possibilities would be 13,824, but the actually occurring combinations number six, of which one is found in only one word. The following diagram represents the permissible three consonant combinations:

Figure 26: Syllable-initial three-consonant combinations

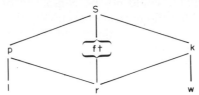

The six three-consonant combinations are, then: /spl/, /spr/, /sfr/, /str/, /skr/, /skw/. The combination /sfr/ occurs only in the word *sphragistics*, the study of engraved seals.

Exercise 8

Find English words to illustrate each of the permissible two-and three-consonant combinations in syllable initial position in English.

Final periphery

We turn now to the rules of phoneme combination that apply to the final periphery of the syllable. Here also it is possible for no consonant to occur: this is the case after any vowel phoneme in English, except the following five, which are always followed by a consonant: /ɛ/, /æ/, /ɒ/, /ʊ/, /ʌ/. All consonant phonemes may occur singly in syllable final position in English, except the following four: /h/, /r/, /w/, /j/. It is more difficult to find precise formulas to express the permissible clusters in syllable final consonant combinations than in syllable initial combinations. As stated earlier, there may be up to four consonants in the final periphery; and as in the case of syllable initial clusters, the fewer are the permissible combinations, the larger the clusters become. Although not expressing the restrictions in the greatest possible detail or with complete precision, the following chart provides a neat representation of permissible combinations in syllable final position:

Figure 27: Syllable-final consonant combinations

Position A	Position B	Position C	Position D
l	Any consonant	θ	t
m n ŋ	except	t d	s
s	h r w j	s z	
k			

Two consonant combinations may comprise either a consonant from Position A combined with a consonant from Position B, or from Position B combined with Position C. The 48 permissible three-consonant syllable final combinations are either Position A + Position B + Position C, or Position B + Position C + Position D. The seven permissible four consonant combinations are as follows: /lkts/, /mpst/, /mpts/, /ksts/, /lfθs/, /ksθs/, /ntθs/, as in *mulcts, glimpsed, tempts, texts, twelfths, sixths, thousandths*. Obviously, these sound clusters are likely to be reduced under the pressures of connected speech. The reader is left with the task of discovering examples for the two-and three-consonant combinations, and indeed of discovering precisely which combinations are found in contemporary English.

The phoneme combination rules that we have been discussing are established on the basis of monosyllabic words. In polysyllabic words it is not always clear, when a number of consonants occurs at syllable boundaries, to which syllable they should be assigned. For example, in the word *extra* /ɛkstrə/ there are obviously two syllables, as two vowel phonemes occur, but it is not clear how the syllables should be divided. Three possible divisions may be made, all of which would give permissible consonant combinations: k-str, ks-tr and kst-r. The method proposed to solve this kind of problem is a statistical one. A statistical survey of syllable initial and syllable final positions has produced an order of 'favoured' syllable beginnings and endings, and the break between syllables that conforms to this most favoured principle is the preferred one. At the beginning of a syllable the order of favour is: CV, VC, CC (C = consonant, V = vowel); at the end of a syllable the order is: VC, CV, CC. So in a word like *aster* /æstə/ (VCCV) the preferred break would be *as-ter*. For *extra* one would presumably have to choose between VC–CCCV and VCCC–CV, ie ɛk-strə and ɛkst-rə.

Stress

Another good reason for recognizing syllables is that there is a further phenomenon that seems to be associated with them, that of **stress** placement. When we hear polysyllabic words spoken we are often aware that some part of the word sounds louder or seems to be uttered with more force than another part. Or, to put it another way, one syllable is more prominent than another. This is achieved by the fact that syllables have different degrees of stress, and this is one of the phonetic factors that ensures that speech does not sound completely monotonous and level. Stress is perceived as difference in loudness, but from the articulatory point of view stress variation arises from force of articulation and more especially from difference in **pitch**.

In English words we usually recognize three degrees of stress: **primary stress**, indicated by a stroke above the line at the beginning of the syllable so stressed ('); **secondary stress**, indicated by a stroke on or below the line at the beginning of the syllable so stressed; and **unstressed syllables**, which are not marked. Each English word, spoken in isolation, has one and only one primary stress. So monosyllables have just a primary stress. In connected speech some monosyllabic words may become unstressed; this applies particularly to 'grammatical' words, those that are also subject to vowel reduction (see Chapter 5). Polysyllabic words may have, though not necessarily, one secondary stress, and in some fairly rare cases two secondary stresses. All remaining syllables will be unstressed. Each English word, then, has a characteristic stress pattern which normally remains unchanged in connected speech.

Unlike in some languages, primary stress in English does not fall on the same syllable in every word (eg last syllable or penultimate); it may fall on just about any syllable. However, for any particular word primary stress usually falls on the same syllable whenever the word occurs. So in every occurrence of *reserve*, primary stress always falls on the second syllable. In English, then, stress placement is free in the sense that there is no uniform pattern for every word, and it is fixed in that the stress patterns of individual words do not change according to context.

Here now are some examples of stress patterns in English polysyllabic words:
secondary + primary ˌun'known
unstressed + primary a'lone
primary + secondary 'proˌfile
primary + unstressed 'ta ble
secondary + unstressed + primary ˌun der'stand
primary + unstressed + unstressed 'ba che lor
primary + unstressed + secondary 'pho toˌgraph
unstressed + primary + unstressed im'por tant
secondary + primary + unstressed ˌun'cer tain
unstressed + primary + two unstressed im'po ssi ble
secondary + primary + two unstressed ˌun'for tu nate
unstressed + primary + unstressed + secondary a'cli maˌtize
primary + three unstressed 'me lan cho ly
primary + unstressed + secondary + unstressed 'e duˌca ted
unstressed + secondary + unstressed + primary misˌun der'stand
unstressed + secondary + unstressed + primary + unstressed conˌsi de'ra tion
secondary + unstressed + primary + unstressed + secondary ˌin ca'pa ciˌtate
unstressed + primary + three unstressed ad'mi nis tra tive
unstressed + secondary + unstressed + primary + two unstressed conˌver ti'bi li ty
secondary + three unstressed + primary + unstressed ˌna tio na li'za tion
secondary + unstressed + primary + three unstressed ˌin dis'tin gui sha ble
secondary + unstressed + secondary + unstressed + primary + two unstressed ˌun reˌli a'bi li ty
unstressed + secondary + two unstressed + primary + two unstressed imˌpe ne tra'bi li ty

A mere difference in stress pattern does not usually serve to distinguish one word from another. Stress is not contrastive in the sense that phonemes are: the substitution of one phoneme for another results in the creation of a different word eg *ban/pan/tan/can* etc. But for stress this is not the case: stress is contrastive in the sense that it contrasts one syllable with another in the linear sequence of a word. However, there is a small number of words in English where the substitution of one stress pattern for another does result in the creation of a different word. Very often, though, the difference in stress pattern is accompanied by a difference in vowel quality, since unstressed syllables tend to be associated with vowel reduction and centralized vowels. Compare the following pairs of words:

'transˌfer	trans'fer
'diˌgest	di'gest
'conˌduct	con'duct
'proˌtest	pro'test

The words in the first column, with primary stress on the first syllable, are nouns; while those in the second column, with primary stress on the second syllable, are verbs.

We have said that each word in English has a characteristic stress pattern. These stress patterns may, however, change in the course of time. For example, the word *momentary* has the stress pattern in modern English of a primary stress on the first syllable, with all the others unstressed. In the seventeenth century the primary stress was on the penultimate syllable, with a secondary stress on the first syllable—*ˌmo men'ta ry*. This older stress pattern is retained in present-day American–English pronunciation. In modern English there are a few words whose stress pattern is variable, even within the speech of an individual, and it could be that these are words whose stress pattern is currently in the course of changing, eg *'in te gral/ˌin'te gral; 'con tro ver sy, con'tro ver sy*.

Exercise 9

Work out the stress patterns for the following English words:
eg *con'trol, 'fant a sy, ˌsup po 'si tion.*

1. machine
2. female
3. magazine
4. quantity
5. telephone
6. rhinoceros
7. cowardliness
8. satisfactory
9. inferiority
10. personification
11. unilateralism

7. Intonation

When we speak, we do not do so on a monotone. Indeed, we should all sound very boring if we did. Speech does not just consist of a sequence of phonemes combined into syllables and words. Accompanying these combinations of phonemes, occurring simultaneously with their articulation, are two features of speech that have linguistic importance. One of these is stress, the importance of which we saw in the previous chapter in contrasting one syllable with another in the phonological structure of words. Stress has a similar function in longer stretches of utterance, in according prominence to one syllable (and so to the word of which it is a part) as against another. For example, the utterance *The cat chased the mouse* could be stressed in one of three ways:

The CAT chased the mouse
The cat CHASed the mouse
The cat chased the MOUSE.

As in the case of words, stress is produced in utterances not especially by greater force of articulation on one syllable rather than another, but more particularly by a change in pitch on a syllable.

Tone groups

The other linguistically important feature accompanying the phoneme combinations is intonation. This is the musical or melodic accompaniment of speech. On the level of intonation each utterance is composed of a number of **tone-groups**. Each tone-group represents a unit of information, which is to say that intonation has the function of dividing an utterance up into information units. Viewed phonetically, tone-groups consist of a series of rises and falls in the pitch of the voice. Since, as we have said, pitch movement is probably the most important contributing factor to stress, intonation and stress can be seen to be closely interconnected in this area of speech production. Besides structuring the utterance in terms of information units, intonation is often important grammatically in distinguishing one type of sentence from another; and it is also important in signalling the attitude of the speaker in what he is saying.

Nucleus

Every tone-group has a **nucleus**, which is its most prominent part. The nucleus is, in other words, the most heavily stressed syllable in a tone-group, and the one which has associated with it a pitch movement. In a tone-group without contrastive or emphatic stress the nucleus falls on the primary stressed syllable of the last lexical word (noun, verb, adjective or adverb, as against pronoun, preposition, etc which are 'grammatical' words—see Chapter 9) eg *The cat chased the MOUSE*. Where there is contrastive or emphatic stress, the primary stressed syllable with such stress is the locus of the nucleus, eg *The cat CHASed the mouse, The CAT chased the mouse.*

Intonation is a notoriously difficult area of phonetic investigation, and phoneticians vary considerably in the way that they analyze it. Among other things, they disagree on the number and types of nucleuses that should be recognized for English. We will restrict ourselves to four types of nucleus, which seems adequate. They are: **falling, rising, falling-rising** and **rising-falling**. We can illustrate these, together with the notation that is frequently used, on the utterance *No*:

Falling `*No* (a matter-of-fact statement)
Rising ,*No* (questioning)
Falling-rising ˅*No* (expressing incredulity)
Rising-falling ˆ*No* (emphatic prohibition, scolding).

The notes in brackets are an attempt to provide a meaning for each of the nucleus tones, and to help the reader identify and produce them for himself.

Tail

Any syllables in a tone-group coming after the nucleus are called the **tail**. The pitch on these syllables continues the direction of the nucleus. So if the nucleus has a rising or a falling-rising pitch, that on the tail will be rising; and it will be falling if the nucleus is falling or rising-falling. Compare the following utterances:

He wants some `*ICE-cream on top of it* (statement)
He wants some ,*ICE-cream on top of it* (questioning).

Head

The part of the tone-group coming directly before the nucleus is called the **head**. This extends from the primary stressed syllable of the first lexical word in the tone-group up to the nucleus. The tones of the head are level, rather than having pitch movement, so that two kinds of effect may be found. The head may all be uttered on the same **pitch**, usually low, or a stepping effect may be produced, either from relatively high to relatively low pitch, or from relatively low to relatively high pitch. Compare the following utterances:

Put it on the `*TABle* (nonchalant instruction)
Put it on the `*TABle* (emphatic, impatient command).

Pre-head

Any syllables coming before the head are called the **pre-head**. They will be part of 'lexical' words or 'grammatical' words, and will be relatively unstressed. The pre-head may normally consist of high level tones or of low level tones. Compare the following utterances:

He doesn't know how to '*SAY it* (matter-of-fact statement)
He doesn't know how to ˆ*SAY it* (mocking tone).

The foregoing is a sketch of one possible way to analyze and describe the intonation of English. When one tries to observe intonation, it is often difficult to recognize what is a falling tone and what is a rising one, but it seems clear that in conversation we do perceive and react to these differences, and that they play an important part in signalling meaning. It is partly from the intonation of an utterance that we understand what a speaker intends by what he is saying. That means his intention both in respect of linguistic meaning, and in respect of his attitude to what he is saying. We will now consider these two aspects of the function of intonation in English.

Intonation and meaning

The contrast between a falling intonation pattern and a rising intonation pattern often correlates with a distinction between a statement and a question. Compare, for example, the intonation patterns that might normally accompany the following:
Cats chase mice.—statement;
Do cats chase mice?—question expecting the answer *yes* or *no*;
Where did the ball go?—question seeking information; it is possible for this kind of question to be spoken with either rising or falling intonation. Indeed, with information seeking questions falling intonation is probably the norm. In any case, for either kind of question it is not just the intonation that indicates whether it is a question or a statement: the order of words (*do* before *cats, did* before *the ball*) and the presence of a question word (*where*) in information seeking questions are enough to make the distinction clear. Where the intonation invariably carries the contrast between statement and question is if the utterance has a statement form but a rising intonation pattern eg *Cats chase mice?*.

Another meaning associated with a rising intonation pattern is that of incompleteness. A rising intonation at the end of a tone-group may indicate that what is being said is not finished, that there is more to come eg

First she went to the cupboard, then she tried the sideboard, and finally she found it in the table drawer.
Or, in offering a list of items—*Would you like tea, or coffee or milk?*—a falling intonation on the last item implies that the choice is limited to those items mentioned, whereas a rising intonation on the last item implies that the list is not closed and that the speaker is open to further suggestions.

The meaning of an utterance may also be affected by where the nucleus of a tone-group is placed: this may be crucial in deciding which items in an utterance belong together grammatically. The by now famous example to illustrate this point is the utterance *He fed her dog biscuits.* If the nucleus falls on *BIScuits*, then it is the dog that he is feeding. If, on the other hand, the nucleus falls on *DOG*, then the lady participant is being fed with dog biscuits.

In a similar way, how the utterance is divided into tone-groups, ie where the tone-group boundaries are placed, may also affect the sense of what is being said. A traditional example is the utterance *He washed and brushed his hair.* If this utterance is spoken as one tone-group, ie with only one nucleus, then it means that the actions referred to applied only to the hair. If, on the other hand, it is spoken as two tone-groups, with a tone-group boundary between *washed* and *and*, then the washing may be taken to refer to other parts of his body and the brushing alone applied to the hair.

Intonation may, then, be a contributory factor in determining which words belong together grammatically in an utterance, by tone-group boundary placement, by the placement of the nucleus within a tone-group, or by the kind of nucleus and general intonation pattern that is used.

Intonation and attitude

Perhaps more important than the use of intonation to make distinctions in grammar is the function of intonation to signal how a speaker intends his utterance to be taken or what his attitude is as he speaks the utterance. But this aspect of intonation is probably the most difficult of all to characterize, not least because we seem not to have a handy or agreed list of labels to apply to different attitudes. For example, how could we characterize the differences between the following utterances:

That's `fine (falling)—? matter of fact
That's ˌfine (rising)—? encouraging
That's ˇfine (falling-rising)—? what have you been worrying about.

Part of the difficulty is that the same intonation pattern may have different meanings or signal different attitudes in different contexts. It seems to depend on the meaning of the lexical items as much as on the meaning of the intonation. Compare the following utterances:

^No (rising-falling)—indignant
^Really (rising-falling)—incredulous, sarcastic
He ^always is (rising-falling)—impatient
and the following:
ˇNo (falling-rising)—doubtful but encouraging
If you ˇwant to (falling-rising)—grudging acceptance.[1]

It is not just the type of nucleus that may be important in conveying the attitude of the speaker, but also the kind of head. For example, *Good Morning* is normally spoken with a falling nucleus on *MORNing*. But the head *good* may be characterized by either a high level pitch or a low level pitch: the high pitch signals the attitude 'cheerful', while the low pitch signals the attitude 'routine'.[2]

Exercise 10

For a normal rendering of the following utterances, consider where the nucleus would fall, and what kind of nucleus it might be:
eg *that's a^STUpid way to do it.*
He'll telephone to `MORrow.

1. Don't do it like that.
2. He came home yesterday.
3. What did he say after that.
4. His suggestion is simply ridiculous.
5. You can't go out.

6. He seems alright to me.
7. Is that all he talked about?
8. He won't find me there.
9. I can't understand it.
10. You're never here on time.

Notes

[1] The attitude labels are taken from A C Gimson's *An introduction to the pronunciation of English* Edward Arnold, 1970.
[2] Labels from Gimson, *op cit.*

For a detailed investigation of the attitudes conveyed by different kinds of tone-group and intonation pattern, the reader is referred to O'Connor, J D, and G F Arnold *Intonation of colloquial English* Longman, 1961.

Part Two: Structures

8. Grammar and sentences

A linguistic description, and consequently a language, is often regarded as being composed of three parts: **phonetics/phonology, grammar** and **semantics**. And there is a sense in which grammar links phonology and semantics: phonemes combine into words (phonology), words combine into sentences (grammar), and sentences refer to events, actions and states in the world (semantics). However, phonology and grammar are different from semantics in that they deal exclusively with the internal structure of language (form), while semantics is concerned largely with the external relationships of language (meaning).

Phonology and grammar

The relationship between phonology and grammar is not as simple as has been implied. There is no automatic progression from phoneme to word to sentence. There are, in fact, two parallel sets of hierarchical relationships: phoneme—syllable—word (—tone-group); morpheme—word—. . .—sentence. It so happens that the unit 'word' occurs in both, and not without reason. 'Word' is the level at which the greatest amount of congruence is found between units in phonology and units in grammar. For the majority of phonological words there are equivalent grammatical words in a one-to-one relationship. But there are several interesting cases that demonstrate the separateness of the two sets of hierarchical relationships. These are cases where there is no one-to-one match between phonological and grammatical word.

The uneven match between phonology and grammar is well illustrated by the so-called **homophones**, where different grammatical words have the same phonemic structure or pronunciation. Take the phonological word /baʊ/. It represents a number of lexical items (grammatical words): *bough, bow* (of a boat), *bow* (verb, 'to incline the head or body'), *bow* (noun, 'inclination of the head or body'). Besides being homophones, the last three items mentioned are also **homographs**, ie they are written the same. Or take the phonological words /stænd/ and /maɪnd/: each of them represents two grammatical words, one a noun and the other a verb. Uneven matching between phonology and grammar is also found the other way round, though more rarely. The past tense of the verb *dream* may be represented phonologically as either /drɛmt/ or /drimd/. And whether *integral* has the phonological structure /ˈɪntəgrəl/ or /ɪnˈtɛgrəl/, it is still the same item as far as the grammar is concerned.

The separateness of the phonological and grammatical sets of relationships is sometimes referred to as the 'double articulation' of language. This implies that language is patterned simultaneously on two levels: sound and syntax. Phonemes pattern into words, words pattern into sentences, and the link between the two levels occurs at the unit 'word'. This, no doubt, accounts for the importance that has been attached to words in the study of language through the centuries, although the status of the word as the basic unit of lexicography (dictionary making) must also be a contributing factor to its importance.

Grammar and dictionary

So grammar is different from phonology: it is concerned with the internal structure of sentences (in terms of words), while phonology is concerned with the way these sentences and words 'sound'. But we need to differentiate grammar from semantics also. If we want to know what a word 'means', we go to a dictionary, where, among other things, we expect to find the 'meaning' or 'definition' of the word we are interested in. Let us say that we came across the sentence *The funnel was raking terribly*, and we wanted to know the meaning of *raking* in this context. What we should look up in the dictionary would be 'rake', not *raking* or *was raking*. And we should find that the meaning was 'of the funnel, slope towards the stern'. Now, in the entry 'rake', some dictionaries would tell you that one of the forms of 'rake' is 'raking', but *raking* would not have a separate entry in the dictionary because it is merely an alternative form of *rake*, not a different 'word'. Here, then, we can distinguish a third sense of the term 'word': the word as an entry in the dictionary, sometimes called a **lexeme**, which may have a number of grammatical forms or words. Thus *big* and *bigger* are distinct words as far as the grammar is concerned, but they are forms of a single lexeme and are both dealt with in a single dictionary entry. Each of the three parts of our linguistic description—phonology, grammar, semantics—deals with 'words', but in each case something slightly different is meant, though of course something common is also implied. We can see, once again, why words have held such an important place in linguistic studies.

Grammar

The grammatical description of a language specifies the way in which sentences in that language may be constructed: it gives the rules of sentence structure. But what is meant by 'rule' here? What is *not* meant by 'rule' is statements of the following kind: 'A preposition is not a suitable word to end a sentence with', or 'It is the height of bad grammar to begin a sentence with 'and', 'but' or a number of other undesirable words'. As in a phonological description, a grammatical description is charting what people actually say rather than what the linguist thinks they ought to say. Now, in the course of doing this for a particular language, the linguist will more than likely find several different usages for one area of grammar or another. But the core of the grammar will probably be the same. Different rules will be found to operate in different regional areas, representing different dialects, and in different kinds of communication: the grammar of scientific textbooks will probably be somewhat different in particular features from that of ordinary conversation or personal letters.

Grammatical descriptions, such as that made by Quirk and his co-authors in *A grammar of contemporary English*, generally define which variety of the language they are describing. This is usually what is called 'general educated usage'. (Variations from this variety may, however, be noted; in *A grammar of contemporary English* attention is paid to the differences between British and American educated usage.)

So grammatical rules are the descriptions of the regular ways in which speakers of a particular language or language variety construct the sentences in that language or variety. They are generalizations of what happens, made from observing many specific instances and relating them to one another. In a sense therefore, there is no such thing as 'bad' grammar. There may be 'inappropriate' grammar, that is, inappropriate for the style of language required for the situation in which it is used. And there may be 'deviant' grammar, when an adult makes a slip of the tongue, or when a child or foreigner has not yet learnt the language completely, or when a poet deliberately produces deviant sentences for effect. Though, of course, you cannot know what is deviant until you know what is normal or accepted!

We use the term 'grammar' in at least two ways, illustrated by the following sentences: *His grammar is terrible, I must go and consult the grammar*. In the first we are referring to the speaker's competence in the language (or lack of it!), that is, what is stored in his brain. In the second we are referring to what a linguist has written, which is a description of the first. This description is not an exact representation of the speaker's grammar (which is what some linguists have suggested). We do not know how our language competence is stored in the brain. We can only make deductions about the system from what people say, and the description is an order, or a model, imposed or inducted by the descriptive linguist.

Grammatical units

From our discussion so far in this chapter, it should be obvious that two grammatical terms have been occurring fairly frequently; they are **word** and **sentence**. In writing, these units are easily recognizable: a word is the unit bounded either side by a space, and the sentence is the unit that stretches from a beginning capital letter to a concluding full-stop. In speech, if such was the only form of language we had, they would be more difficult to identify, but the fact that they occur in writing implies that the native speaker has some intuitive awareness of what is a word and what is a sentence in his language.

In a sense, these two units—word and sentence—are basic to grammar, though they are by no means the only units of grammatical structure, and there is no direct relation between words and sentences. Neither are they the smallest and largest units of grammar respectively: there are recognizable units smaller than words, and units larger than sentences. However, sentences do exhibit a structure that no larger unit, eg paragraph or discourse, does. And larger units are discussed in terms of changes that take place in sentences or of characteristic features of particular sentences: this is the area of **textsyntax** which we shall be considering in Chapters 15 and 16. The units smaller than words are called **morphemes,** which we shall be considering in Chapters 17 and 18. For the present let the following examples serve

as illustrations of the decomposability of words:
nation—al—ize—d, tempt—ation—s, un—sympathe—tic, re—paint—ing.

Phrase and clause

Now let us consider the statement made in the previous paragraph, that words do not pattern directly into sentences. This implies that there are some intervening levels of organization between word and sentence. Consider the following sentence: *The grand old man of letters stumbled along the dimly lit road, but the pen which he had lost had been picked up by a small boy.* This sentence cannot be viewed simply as a concatenation of words: *The + grand + old + man + . . .* etc. Some groups of words belong more closely together than any of them do with any others, and these longer stretches of word groups in turn form larger units. In this sentence we can recognize the following word groupings: *the grand old man of letters, along the dimly lit road, the pen which he had lost, had been picked up, by a small boy*; and *stumbled* belongs on its own. These word groupings combine in turn into the following larger units: *the grand old man of letters stumbled along the dimly lit road* and *the pen which he had lost had been picked up by a small boy.* And then these two units are linked together by *but* to form the complete sentence.

The intervening units between word and sentence are usually called **phrase** and **clause**: phrases are equivalent to the 'word groupings' of the previous paragraph, and clauses to the 'larger units'. So words pattern into phrases, phrases into clauses, and clauses into sentences. Or, from the alternative perspective, a sentence is composed of one or more clauses, a clause is composed of one or more phrases, and a phrase is composed of one or more words. So the instruction *Fire!* is one word, one phrase, one clause, one sentence. Our investigation of grammar will, then, be concerned with the kinds of words, phrases, clauses and sentences that occur in contemporary English, and with the rules for their structure and combination.

Finally, in this chapter, we must consider ways of representing the structure of sentences. There are two conventional methods: bracketing, and tree diagrams. In this book we shall be using tree diagrams, because they are easier to read and decipher. But below, for illustration, are the bracketing and tree diagram for the following sentence 'S' stands for sentence, 'Cl' for clause, 'Ph' for phrase, and 'Wd' for word: *John kicked the ball and Harry caught it.*

Bracketing: S(Cl(Ph(Wd:John))(Ph(Wd:kicked)) (Ph(Wd:the)(Wd:ball))) and
(Cl(Ph(Wd:Harry))(Ph(Wd:caught))(Ph(Wd:it)))

Figure 28: Tree diagram

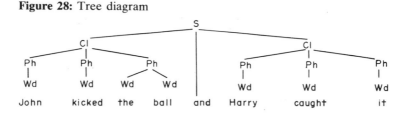

Now here are the tree diagrams for three more sentences.

The fifty English tourists walked along the Great wall

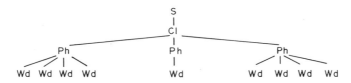

If you write to this address they will send you a coloured brochure

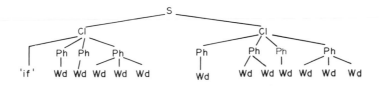

The old lady has been anxious about her cats

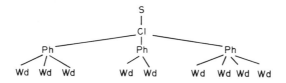

Exercise 11

Analyze the following sentences into clauses, phrases and words, representing your analysis by means of a tree diagram.

1. Go away!
2. Jim sold his bicycle to a friend.
3. Martha loves cats.
4. The two men were fishing for trout in the clear stream beside the woodman's cottage.
5. The committee elected the oldest member president for the coming year.
6. Your apple pie looks really delicious.
7. Young Jim has been looking for tadpoles in the village pond.
8. She gave him a look which betokened trouble.
9. Old Mother Hubbard went to the cupboard to fetch her poor dog a bone.
10. When she got there the cupboard was bare, and so the poor dog had none.

9. Word classes

One of the traditional ways of analyzing a sentence was known as 'parsing'. This involved identifying each word in the sentence and assigning it to the appropriate 'part of speech', and saying what 'form' the word had. For example, in the sentence *The cows are in the field, cows* would belong to the part of speech called noun, and it would be in the 'plural' form; *are* would be a verb, and have the third person plural form of the infinitive *be*; and so on.

This kind of analysis derived from techniques used in the investigation of the classical languages, Latin and Greek, where the endings of words give a good deal of information about the syntactic function of words, ie their particular job in the sentence. For instance, in the Latin sentence *Puer amat puellam* ('the boy loves the girl'), *puer* and *puellam* are identified as subject and object of the sentence respectively simply because their endings (or lack of them in the case of *puer*) assign them to a particular 'case' (nominative and accusative respectively), which is a mark of syntactic function (subject or object). The particular kind of endings, in the case of *puer* and *puellam* case endings, also indicate which part of speech the word belongs to.

Since English does not have such an elaborate case system as Latin or Greek, a parsing of English sentences does not yield nearly so much syntactic information. Besides, underlying the technique of parsing is the notion that sentences are made up of strings of words, and that each word has a function in the sentence identifiable from its form. There is, then, no notion of intervening levels, such as phrase and clause.

Definitions

However, the notion of 'part of speech' is still a useful one, though the term **word class** is usually preferred these days. It is convenient to talk about classes of words that have some characteristic or other in common. Deciding which characteristics should be regarded as defining characteristics for a particular word class is not easy. Traditionally, the parts of speech had a 'notional' definition; for example, a noun was defined as 'the name of a person, place or thing', or a verb was called a 'doing word'. While these definitions have some validity, they were nevertheless too loose and restricted to be very serviceable in a rigorous analysis. For example, in the sentence *His thumps became louder*, 'thump' hardly falls into the definition of noun as 'the name of a person, place or thing', it seems rather to be a 'doing word'; and *became* can hardly be called a 'doing word', since it refers to a quite passive process.

For the purposes of a 'scientific' definition, a more watertight set of characteristics was looked for, and these were found in the grammatical characteristics of words.

For example, a noun is often defined as a word that typically inflects for plural number (*cow—cows*), functions as head of a noun phrase (see Chapter 10), which typically functions as subject or object of a clause (see Chapter 13). In other words, the definitions of the word classes looked more to the internal structure of language, rather than to the relation between language and the external world.

Now, while such a form of words as we have given for a noun above may go some way towards providing a watertight definition of the word class, it does not always help very much in aiding the recognition of different types of words. For this, a notional characterization is far easier to apply, and it is certainly possible to improve on the notional definitions of traditional grammar. We could say, for example, that a noun generally refers to 'things' in the broadest sense, whether objects (*table*), activities (*his hammering*), feelings (*hatred*), ideas (*eternity*), as well as people and places.

Open and closed classes

Word classes are generally divided into two broad groups: those which are **open classes** and those which are **closed classes**. These terms refer to the membership of the classes. For the closed classes the membership is fixed; it is in general not possible to add new members. For the open classes the opposite is the case: new members are being constantly added, as new words are coined in science, technology, or by advertisers or sub-cultures. The open classes of words are: **noun, verb, adjective, adverb**; the closed classes are: **pronoun, numeral, determiner, preposition, conjunction**. It will be clear that the open classes bear the greatest load in terms of meaning, in the sense of reference to things in the world, while the function of the closed classes is oriented more towards internal linguistic relationships, though this is by no means exclusively the case. Numerals obviously refer to quantity in the external world, and prepositions refer to relations in time and space.

Nouns

Nouns, as we have said, generally refer to 'things' in the broadest sense. If we have a noun for something, it implies that we view it as a 'thing' (a process known as 'reification'). For example, in English we have nouns for *thunder* and *lightning*, whereas in Hopi, a North-American Indian language, these concepts can only be expressed by verbs.

The class of nouns is traditionally divided into a number of subclasses. There is, first of all, a division into **proper** nouns and **common** nouns. Proper nouns refer to unique 'things', such as people, places or institutions eg *Robert Walpole, Cologne, The Guardian*. Common nouns do not refer to unique things: the noun *plant* does not refer to a unique object, but either to a class of objects or to a specific instance of that class. Common nouns are often subdivided into **concrete** nouns and **abstract** nouns. Concrete nouns refer to perceivable objects in the world, while abstract nouns refer to ideas, feelings, and 'things' of that kind. So *table, bear, tree* would be concrete nouns; and *truth, love, imagination* would be abstract nouns.

A division which cuts across that between concrete and abstract nouns is the division between **countable** and **mass** (or uncountable) nouns. Countable nouns, as the label suggests, refer to objects that may be counted, objects of which there may be more than one, eg *box, six boxes*. Mass nouns are in principle uncountable, eg *flour, bread, cheese, wine*. Some nouns may, in fact, be both countable and mass, depending on the context in which they are being used, eg *cake* is a mass noun in *He wants some cake* but a countable noun in *She has baked six cakes*. And some mass nouns may be used as if they were countable nouns eg *cheese* in *these five cheeses from Switzerland* or *wine* in *those six wines of Alsace*; but the meaning is not simply a plurality of objects, but rather 'a number of kinds of objects', ie five kinds of cheese and six kinds of wine. Mass nouns like *flour* and *bread* can only be made countable by prefixing some expression of measurement eg *six spoonsful of flour, five loaves of bread*.

Verbs

Verbs generally refer to actions, events and processes eg *give, happen, become*. They typically have a number of distinct forms: infinitive (*(to) walk*), third person singular present tense (*walks*), past tense (*walked*), present participle (*walking*), past participle (*walked*). The past participle is usually the same as the past tense form, but for some verbs it is different eg *show* has past tense *showed* and past participle *shown*; similarly *give* has *gave* and *given* respectively.

The main division made among verbs is that between **auxiliary** verbs and **lexical** verbs. Auxiliary verbs are a closed subclass and have a mainly grammatical function. The subclass of auxiliary verbs includes *be, have* and *do* in certain of the uses of these verbs, and additionally the modal verbs, ie *can, could, will, would, shall, should, may, might, must* and one or two others.

Among lexical verbs a distinction is traditionally made between **transitive** and **intransitive** verbs: transitive verbs are those that require an 'object' (see Chapter 13), while intransitive verbs are those that do not take an object. Thus, *go* is an intransitive verb, since we cannot say 'He went something' or 'What did he go?; while *thump* is a transitive verb, since we can say *Jim thumped Michael* and *Who/What did Jim thump?*. A number of verbs are both transitive and intransitive, depending on the context, eg *march* is intransitive in *The soldiers marched to the barracks* but transitive in *The captain marched the soldiers to the barracks*.

A further, more notional distinction is made among lexical verbs, the distinction between **dynamic** verbs and **stative** verbs. Syntactically, the dynamic verbs may enter the *be* + -ing construction eg *They are speaking Russian*; whereas the stative verbs may not eg 'They are knowing Russian'. *Speak* is, then, a dynamic verb, but *know* is a stative verb.

Dynamic verbs may be further subdivided notionally into **Activity** verbs (*drink, play, write*), **process** verbs (*grow, widen*), verbs of **bodily sensation** (*ache, feel, itch*), **transitional event** verbs (*arrive, die, fall*), and **momentary** verbs (*hit, jump, kick*). And stative verbs are divided further into verbs of **inert perception** and **cognition** (*astonish, believe, imagine, like*) and **relational** verbs (*belong to, contain, matter*).

Adjectives

Adjectives typically amplify the meaning of a noun, either by occurring immediately before it, as in *the wide road*, or by being linked to it by means of a **copula** verb, as in *The road is/became wide*. For this reason adjectives are often characterized as descriptive words.

Like verbs, adjectives may be divided into a **dynamic** and a **stative** subclass; but whereas verbs are typically dynamic, adjectives are typically stative. *Tall* is a stative adjective, as in *Jim is tall; careful* is a dynamic adjective, as in *Jim is being careful*.

A further subclassification of adjectives is that into **gradable** and **non-gradable** adjectives. Gradable adjectives may be modified by certain adverbs that indicate the intensity of what the adjective refers to eg *very careful, more beautiful*. Most adjectives are gradable, but some are not eg *previous, shut*. It is not possible to say 'his more previous visit' or 'The door was very shut'.

One further distinction sometimes made is that between **inherent** and **non-inherent** adjectives. Inherent adjectives, which are the majority, characterize the referent of the noun directly eg *a wooden cross, a new car*. Non-inherent adjectives, or non-inherent uses of adjectives do not exhibit a direct characterization of the noun eg *a wooden actor, a new friend*. In this case the actor is not made of wood, and the friend is not just created or produced.

Adverbs

Adverbs represent a very diverse set of words. There are basically two kinds; those which refer to circumstantial information about the action, event or process, such as the time, the place or the manner of it, and those which serve to intensify other adverbs and adjectives. The first group may be illustrated by the following: *yesterday, now; there, outside; carefully, beautifully* and the second group by *very* as in *very hard, extremely* as in *extremely uncomfortable, terribly* as in *terribly quietly*. The composition of the class of adverbs and their function will become clearer when we discuss the adverb phrase in Chapter 12 and the adverbial clause in Chapter 14.

We turn now to the closed classes. Here there is less need for a notional definition, since very often the words involved have little or no reference to external reality, and in any case the exhaustive membership of each class could be listed. We will attempt a characterization of each class, nevertheless.

Pronouns

Pronouns, as the name implies, have the main function of substituting for nouns, once a noun has been mentioned in a particular text.

There are several subclasses. The central subclass is that of **personal** pronouns (*I, me, you, he, him, she, her, it, we, us, they, them*), along with the **reflexive** pronouns (*myself, yourself, himself* etc) and the **possessive** pronouns (*mine, yours, his, hers, its, ours, theirs*). With these pronouns a distinction is made between first, second and third person, that is between speaker (*I*), addressee (*you*), and other (*he*), and also between singular and plural number (*I—we, he—they* etc). The singular/plural distinction does not, however, operate for second person (*you*), which refers to just one or to more than one addressee.

Another subclass is that of **interrogative** pronouns. These substitute in questions not only for nouns, but also for adjectives and adverbs. This subclass includes *who, what, which, how, when, where, why*, as in the following examples: *Who were you talking to?, What is the time?, Which train are you catching?, How did the accident happen?, When are you going on holiday?, Where have you left your umbrella?, Why did you hit your sister?*.

Relative pronouns substitute for nouns as elements in relative clauses (see Chapter 10) and include *who, which, whose, that* and *whom*; eg *the boy who has lost his ball* . . ..

Demonstrative pronouns also substitute for nouns, but they imply a gesture of pointing, either to something in the situational context, or to some previous or following language eg **That** *is an interesting point,* **This** *is a beautiful picture.* The subclass of demonstrative pronouns includes *this, that, these, those*. Finally, there is a subclass of **indefinite** pronouns, among which are included *all, many, few, everyone, anything, nothing* etc. Again, they substitute for nouns but at the same time express an indefinite quantity of some 'thing'.

Numerals

Numerals are of two kinds; **ordinal** and **cardinal**. Ordinal numerals, as the name indicates, specify the order of an item and comprise the series *first, second, third, fourth* and so on. Cardinal numerals do not specify order, but merely quantity, and comprise the series *one, two, three, four* etc.

Determiners

Determiners are a class of words that are used with nouns and have the function of defining the reference of the noun in some way. The class is divided into two broad groups, **identifiers** and **quantifiers**. The subclass of identifiers includes the **articles**, ie the **indefinite** article *a/an* and the **definite** article *the*; the **possessives** *my, your, his, her, its, our, their*; and the **demonstratives** *this, that, these, those*. The last two groups are often called **possessive** adjectives and **demonstrative** adjectives, to distinguish them from the possessive and demonstrative pronouns. Demonstratives in fact have the same class membership as demonstrative pronouns. The identifiers may be illustrated by the following examples: *a book, the cow, my pencil, those sheep*. Quantifiers are expressions of indefinite quantity, and this class has some members in common with that of indefinite pronouns. Among the quantifers are included *a lot of, many, few, several, little* etc, and they may be illustrated by the following examples: *a lot of cheese, few ideas, little comfort*.

Prepositions

Prepositions have as their chief function that of relating a noun phrase to another unit. The relationship may be one of **time** (eg *after the meal*), **place** (eg *in front of the bus*) or **logic** (eg *because of his action*). Many prepositions may be used to express more than one of these relationships eg *from* in *from the beginning, from the house, from his words.*

The other function of prepositions is to be tied to a particular verb or adjective and to link that verb or adjective with its object. In this case the preposition cannot be said to have any special meaning of its own eg *for* in *They are waiting for the bus,* and *about* in *He is anxious about his future.*

Conjunctions

Conjunctions, as their name implies, also have a joining function, usually that of joining one clause to another, but sometimes also of one noun to another. They are of two kinds: **co-ordinating** conjunctions, such as *and, or, but*, which join two items on an equal footing; and **subordinating** conjunctions, such as *when, if, why, whether, because, since,* which subordinate one item to another in some way. The subordination may be one of time, as in *He will come when he is ready*, or one of reason, as in *He cannot come, because he is ill,* or some other kind (see further Chapter 14).

Exercise 12
Identify the word class (noun, verb, adjective, adverb, pronoun, numeral, determiner, preposition, conjunction abbreviated to N, V, adj, adv, pron, num, det, prep, conj) to which each word in the following sentences belongs.
eg After (conj) they (pron) had (V) visited (V) the (det) British (adj) Museum, (N) the (det) twenty (num) foreign (adj) visitors (N) made (V) their (det) way (N) quickly (adv) to (prep) the (det) Houses (N) of (prep) Parliament (N).

1. When April with his sweet showers has pierced the drought of March to the root, then people wish to go on pilgrimages.
2. Hardly knowing what she did, she picked up a little bit of stick, and held it out to the puppy.
3. Alice looked at the jury-box, and saw that, in her haste, she had put the Lizard in head downwards, and the poor little thing was waving its tail about in a melancholy way, being quite unable to move.
4. To gain the maximum amount of fruit from a strawberry bed a certain amount of attention is needed now.
5. By this time of year most of us are viewing our flower borders with a fairly critical eye, noting spaces where improvements can be made.

10. Phrases 1—noun phrases

Types of phrase

In Chapter 8 we saw that words did not combine directly to form sentences, but that there were two intermediate levels of syntactic organization. Words pattern into phrases. This means that phrases may be described in terms of the kinds or classes of words that function in them, and of the order in which the words or classes of words are arranged relative to each other. Five types of phrase are recognized in English: **noun phrase, verb phrase, adjective phrase, adverb phrase,** and **prepositional phrase**. The first four of these take their name from the word that is the chief word or **head** of the phrase. The prepositional phrase is different in that there is no head word. For the other types of phrase the minimal form of the phrase is the head. For example, in the clause *Lions become ferocious nightly*, we have a noun, verb, adjective, adverb sequence; and each of these words is in turn the sole constituent and head of the corresponding phrase, ie noun phrase, verb phrase, adjective phrase and adverb phrase. A prepositional phrase, on the other hand, is always composed of two elements, a preposition and a noun, or rather noun phrase, eg *at night, in the jungle*. In this chapter we shall be considering the structure of noun phrases, in the following one the structure of verb phrases, and in Chapter 12 the structure of adjective phrases, adverb phrases and prepositional phrases.

Noun phrase

The noun phrase in English is composed potentially of three parts. The central part of the noun phrase, the **head**, is obligatory: it is the minimal requirement for the occurrence of a noun phrase. The other two parts are optionally occurring. The head may be preceded by some **pre-modification**, and it may be followed by some **post-modification**. For example, in the noun phrase *that old car in the drive*, *car* constitutes the head—it is the primary reference of the phrase; *that old* is the pre-modification, and *in the drive* the post-modification.

Heads

The most usual kind of head of a noun phrase is a **noun**, like *car* in the example above. Alternatively, the head may be a pronoun of some kind, very commonly a personal pronoun, eg *he* in *He is there*. Other kinds of pronoun functioning as head of a noun phrase include: indefinite pronoun, eg *someone* in *Someone called*; possessive pronoun, eg *mine* in *Mine are green*; demonstrative pronoun, eg *this* in *This beats everything*. When a pronoun functions as head of a noun phrase, it usually occurs without any kind of modification: pre-modification is virtually impossible for pronouns, though post-modification may occasionally be found, eg *he who hesitates.* There is also a restriction on the modification that may be found with proper nouns, ie those referring to unique persons and things: again post-modification is possible, while pre-modification rarely occurs, eg *Lovely Morecambe, which we visited last year.*

Pre-modification

The pre-modification in a noun phrase consists of a number of word classes or sub-classes in a specific order: **identifier—numeral/quantifier—adjective—noun modifier**, as for example in the noun phrase *these five charming country cottages.*

The class of **identifiers** includes articles ('a', 'the'), demonstratives ('this', 'that') and possessives ('my', 'your', 'his', etc); and they come before any numerals or indefinite quantifiers that may be present, eg *those fifty postage stamps, the many enquiries, her first attempt.* Only one identifier may occur in any noun phrase; that is to say, articles, demonstratives and possessives are mutually exclusive in English. It is not possible to say 'the my book' or the like; and the sequence *this my book* in fact consists of two noun phrases in apposition, with *this* being a demonstrative pronoun functioning as head of the first noun phrase: indeed, in writing, it would be usual to write the sequence with a comma between the two noun phrases—*this, my book.* If one wishes to combine article or demonstrative identifier with possessive, then an 'of'-phrase with the possessive pronoun must be used, eg *the/this book of mine.*

More than one **numeral/quantifier** may, however, occur in a noun phrase, though there is a restricted number of possible combinations. Favourite sequences are ordinal numeral (especially 'first' and 'last') + indefinite quantifier, eg *the first few hours*; ordinal + cardinal, eg *the second five days*; and indefinite quantifier + cardinal numeral (especially round numbers), eg *several thousand people, many scores of ants.*

There is a small group of words which may occur before the identifier in a noun phrase, which are sometimes called **pre-determiners.** They also have a quantifier reference, and the most common members of this class are 'all', 'both' and 'half', together with fraction numerals ('one-third of', etc); eg *both/all the desperate terrorists.* The linguistic function of the identifiers is to indicate the status of the noun phrase in relation to its linguistic and situational context: this is basically a textual function, and we shall return to consider the identifiers from this point of view in more detail in Chapter 16.

Adjectives, whose function is to amplify the head noun in some way, come after the identifiers and numerals/quantifiers. Several adjectives, or none at all, may occur in a noun phrase, and when a number of adjectives do occur there appears to be some principle of ordering at work. For example, native speakers regard *the big red fox* as grammatical, but *the red big fox* as deviant. Likewise in the following noun phrase, the order given appears to be the normal one and any deviation from it is in some way abnormal; *a charming small round old brown French oaken writing desk.* It is often assumed that the ordering is according to the semantic category of the adjective, although it is not clear that this is necessarily always the case or that the ordering is entirely rigid. In the above example the categories represented are*: 1. epithet (*charming*), 2. size (*small*), 3. shape (*round*), 4. age (*old*), 5. colour (*brown*), 6. origin (*French*), 7. substance (*oaken*), 8. present participle (*writing*); and then these might be followed by other adjectives of the type *medical* and *social*, which are denominal (ie derived from nouns). It is, of course, unusual for all the possible positions to be filled, except in a linguist's concocted example!

Between adjectives and the head noun come **noun modifiers**. Thus nouns may function not only as heads of noun phrases, but also as modifiers in the noun phrase, eg *a country garden*, *the village policeman*, *the news agency*. It is unusual for more than one noun modifier to occur in a noun phrase (cf *the village action group*): in a noun phrase like *the child safety harness*, *child* modifies the whole of *safety harness*, so that *harness* is modified in the first instance by just *safety*; similarly in the noun phrase *the child poverty action group*, *child* modifies *poverty*, and *child poverty* together with *action* modify *group*. Noun modifier + head noun constructions are often the first stage in the formation of compound nouns (see Chapter 18). A word like *flycatcher* probably started off as *fly catcher* (ie noun modifier + noun) before progressing, in writing at least, to *fly-catcher* and ultimately to *flycatcher*; cf *armchair*, *lifestory*, *dishcloth*.

There is one further kind of pre-modifier that we have not yet mentioned and which we did not include in the earlier list. This is a **noun phrase in the genitive case**, appearing in the pre-modification of another noun phrase, eg *this delightful old gentleman's scruffy bowler hat*. This is analyzed as: noun phrase genitive (*this delightful old gentleman's*), adjective (*scruffy*), noun modifier (*bowler*), head noun (*hat*). Noun phrases in the genitive are marked by an *'s* added to their final word, and often, though not always, indicate possession; for this reason they are more commonly found with animate nouns as head than inanimate nouns (cf *the ship's red funnel*, *?the bicycle's low saddle*, *?the car's open window*). The noun phrase genitive may be considered to be substituting for a possessive identifier (*my*, *your*, *her*, etc) in the noun phrase in which it occurs as pre-modifier, eg in the example above *his scruffy bowler hat*. Clearly, the noun phrase genitive may in turn be subject to analysis like any other noun phrase, eg *this* (identifier), *delightful* (adjective), *old* (adjective), *gentleman* (head noun), *'s* (genitive marker).

Exercise 13
Make an analysis of the following noun phrases in terms of the word classes that they comprise.
eg Those (ident) delicious (adj) ice-creams (head); my brother's (NP gen) first (num) two (num) nephews (head); my (ident) brother (head) 's (gen)
 1. Five green bottles
 2. My third currant bun
 3. Jim's many fatal mistakes
 4. All our many grievous sins
 5. An ugly large yellow submarine
 6. Plenty of delicious rice pudding
 7. This mischievous tax collector's grabbing hand
 8. His underrated musical talent
 9. Her blue collapsible silk umbrella
10. All our relations' dirty screaming offspring.

Post-modification

The post-modification position in a noun phrase is most commonly filled not by specific word classes or subclasses, but by phrases or clauses. Three kinds of phrasal/clausal post-modification occur: **relative clauses, non-finite clauses,** and **prepositional phrases**. Additionally, it is possible for an **adjective** or an **adverb** to function as a post-modifier in a noun phrase.

Adjective post-modification is found usually with indefinite pronouns as head: these cannot be pre-modified by adjectives; eg *something strange, somebody brave*. Adjectives do not normally come after nouns, except in a few set phrases (probably copied from French), eg *blood royal, heir apparent*. **Adverbs** are rather more frequently found as post-modifiers in noun phrases, eg *the time before, the room above, the morning after, the bus behind*. These examples could possibly be regarded as reductions of a prepositional phrase, eg *the time before this one, the room above us*; and it seems that the most usual kind of post-modifying adverb is one that may function alternatively as a preposition (eg *back, in front (of), below,* etc).

A **relative clause**, which is discussed further in Chapter 14, is a full clause, one of whose members (ie phrases) consists of a relative pronoun as head, which refers back to the head noun of the noun phrase in which it occurs as a post-modifier. For example, in the noun phrase *the man who came here yesterday*, the relative clause is *who came here yesterday*, with *who* as the relative pronoun which refers back to the head *man*, and which is the subject noun phrase (see Chapter 13) within the relative clause. Compare this with the noun phrase *the man who(m) I saw yesterday*, where *who(m)* is a relative pronoun functioning as object in the relative clause. The relative pronouns *who* and *whom* are used to stand for heads that refer to persons; *which* is used for non-humans, and *that* may be used for both. In addition, there is a 'genitive' relative pronoun *whose*, as in *the man whose car was stolen*, which functions like an NP genitive within one of the noun phrases of the relative clause. *Whose* is generally regarded as the genitive form of *who* (ie = *of whom*), but it may also be used with non-human head nouns, eg *the car whose windows were broken*. Some native speakers, however, prefer to avoid *whose* with non-human heads, but the alternative (*of which*) sounds formal and cumbersome, eg *the car the windows of which were broken* or *the car of which the windows were broken*. If the relative pronoun is functioning as object in the relative clause, then it may be omitted, eg *the man I saw yesterday*, where the relative clause is *who(m)/that I saw yesterday*.

A further type of relative clause is one involving comparison, eg *She buys more clothes in a month than I buy in a year*. Here the relative clause is the *than*-clause, and the equivalent of the relative pronoun is the *than*, which refers back to the quantifier *more* in the noun phrase. In the clause *She buys more expensive clothes than she can afford*, the *more* expresses the comparative degree of the adjective, and the *than* now refers back to the comparative adjective. A superlative adjective as pre-modifier may be followed by a relative clause introduced by *that*, eg *the most expensive clothes (that) she can afford*: in this instance, as the *that* functions as object in the relative clause, it may be omitted.

Non-finite clauses are clauses usually without subjects, introduced by a non-finite form of the verb. There are, therefore, three kinds of non-finite clause, according to the form of the verb that introduces them: **infinitive clause**, eg *to answer this question*; **present participle clause**, eg *coming down the road*; and **past participle clause**, eg *expected to arrive at any moment*. Besides being able to substitute for noun phrases as subject or more usually object of a clause (see Chapter 14), non-finite clauses may function in the post-modification of a noun phrase, eg in the following noun phrases: *the man to answer this question; the car coming down the road*; *the woman expected to arrive at any moment*. Non-finite clauses can often be regarded as reductions of relative clauses, eg *the man who should answer this question, the car which is coming down the road, the woman who is expected to arrive at any moment*. It will be noted that the present participle clause relates to a progressive form ('be' + -ing) of the verb, and the past participle clause to a passive form ('be' + -ed) in the relative clause (see Chapter 11 for explanation of 'progressive' and 'passive'). While a past participle clause is always linked to a passive and is thus restricted to transitive verbs, a present participle clause is not always relatable to a progressive form, though it always relates to an active; eg *Someone knowing the circumstances* is related to *someone who knows the circumstances*, not to 'someone who is knowing . . .'.

For present and past participle clauses as post-modifiers in noun phrases the implied subject is the head of the noun phrase, ie *the car* in *the car coming down the road*, *the woman* in *the woman expected to arrive at any moment*. For infinitive clauses, however, the implied subject is not always the head of the noun phrase. Clearly it is so in *the man to answer this question*; but not in *the man to ask about this question*, which can be related to something like *Everybody/You should ask the man about this question*. It is also possible to insert a specific subject by means of a *for*-phrase, eg *a good man for Harry to see about his problem*.

The most frequently occurring kind of post-modifier in a noun phrase is a **prepositional phrase**, the structure of which is discussed in Chapter 12. Examples of post-modifying prepositional phrases are: *the man after me*, in which *after me* is the prepositional phrase as post-modifier; *the man in the queue on the boat*, in which *in the queue on the boat* is post-modifier to *man*, and *on the boat* is post-modifier to *queue*. The full range of prepositions is used to introduce post-modifying prepositional phrases. Like non-finite clauses, prepositional phrases may be related to a fuller relative clause, very often with the verb *be*, eg *the man who is after me, the man who is in the queue which is on the boat*. Verbs other than *be* are, however, implied in *the newspaper as a propaganda instrument, the man of the hour, the girl with freckles*.

One striking fact about these different kinds of phrasal/clausal post-modification emerging from our discussions is the degree of explicitness associated with each of them. As one passes from relative clauses through non-finite clauses to prepositional phrases, so one finds a gradation from most to least explicit; cf *the cow which is standing in the meadow, the cow standing in the meadow, the cow in the meadow*.

Exercise 14

Analyse the following noun phrases in terms of the word classes or subclasses or other kinds of phrase or clause that comprise them.

eg the (ident) bleak (adj) landscape (head) covered in snow (post-mod non-fin cl); the (ident) sixth (num) ballpoint (N mod) pen (head) that I have broken (post-mod rel cl).

1. the old cupboard with the blue handles
2. all the coal stacked outside the back door
3. the third unpleasant task to be assigned to me
4. the fourth place behind Jim
5. the major upset of the year
6. the clearest instructions that anybody could have been given
7. this sudden disaster approaching us
8. all the eighty elderly passengers in the front coach
9. several irate gentleman farmers waiting for the prime minister
10. a poor little boy who seems to be lost.

Note

* These categories are based on those in R A Close's *A Reference Grammar for Students of English* Longman, 1975.

11. Phrases 2—verb phrases

Structure

In the verb phrase all the elements are verbs of one kind or another. In Chapter 9 we made a distinction between auxiliary verbs and lexical verbs. A verb phrase contains one lexical verb as **head** and may have up to four auxiliary verbs, besides the negative word *not*, as **modifiers**. The lexical verb is always the last element in the verb phrase; eg *may not have been being interrogated*, in which the lexical verb is *interrogate* and the other elements auxiliary verbs together with *not*.

The **lexical verb** carries the primary reference of the verb phrase, relating to an action, process or event in extralinguistic reality. The lexical verb may be composed of more than one (orthographic or phonological) word, especially in the case of **'phrasal'** and **'prepositional' verbs**. For example, in the sequence *she is looking after her aged mother*, the lexical verb is most conveniently considered to be *look after*. And in the sequence *he must have looked up the word in the dictionary*, the lexical verb is *look up*. *Look after* is an example of a prepositional verb: the preposition is the only one possible in the context and it always comes immediately after the verb word. *Look up*, on the other hand, is a phrasal verb: the adverb particle *up* may come either before or after an object which is a noun, cf *he must have looked the word up*; and it must come after if the object is a pronoun, eg *he must have looked it up* not 'he must have looked up it'. Multi-word verbs also include so-called **phrasal–prepositional** verbs, which include both an adverb particle and a preposition, eg *put up with*, *look down on*.

Among **auxiliary verbs** we distinguish between primary auxiliaries (*be*, *have*, *do*) and modal auxiliaries (*can*, *may*, *will*, *must*, etc.). Auxiliary verbs serve to realize the grammatical categories associated with the verb phrase, especially tense, aspect and mood (see below for discussion of these categories). The modal auxiliary, of which there may be only one in a verb phrase, always comes first if it is present and is followed by the infinitive (without *to*) form of the verb, eg *he may come*, *they can stay*. The negative word always takes up second position. The primary auxiliary *be* has two uses; *have* has one. *Be* is followed by the present participle (*-ing* form of the verb) to indicate **progressive** (alternatively called **continuous**) **aspect**, as in *he is coming*, *she was going*. *Be* is followed by the past participle (*-ed* form of the verb) to indicate **passive voice**, as in *it is finished*, *it was eaten*. *Have* is followed by the past participle (*-ed* form of the verb) to indicate **perfect** or **perfective aspect**, as in *he has gone*, *they had eaten*.

When combinations of auxiliary verbs occur, the verb form that a particular auxiliary requires is taken by the verb immediately following the auxiliary in question, whether that verb is a lexical verb or an auxiliary verb. The relative order among auxiliary verbs is as follows:

modal—*have*—*be* (progressive)—*be* (passive).

And the forms they require are, then, as follows: modal requires infinitive, *have* requires past participle, *be* (progressive) requires present participle, and *be* (passive) requires past participle. Which form the lexical verb has, depends on the immediately preceding auxiliary.

Here are some examples of verb phrases with combinations of auxiliary verbs:

he has been going (*have*-perfective + *be*-progressive)
he had been being examined (*have*-perfective + *be*-progressive +
    be-passive)
he will not have been being interviewed (modal + negative +
    have-perfective + *be*-progressive + *be*-passive).

The first auxiliary in a verb phrase is called the **operator**, and has a number of special functions:

1. The operator is the element in the verb phrase that is marked for **tense**; that is, the distinction between 'past' and 'present' (see below). If there is no auxiliary in the verb phrase, then the lexical verb itself is marked for tense. Examples: *he is coming, he was coming*; *she has gone, she had gone*; *he walks, he walked*.
2. The operator changes places with the subject of a clause in most questions; for example, *is she coming?*, *What has she been doing?*, *Where will she be coming from?*, but cf *Who has seen her?* where the *wh*-word (interrogative pronoun) is the subject of the clause and comes first like all *wh*-interrogatives.
3. The negative word *not* is placed immediately after the operator and before any other auxiliaries; for example, *he has not come, she may not be staying*. A contracted form of the negative word may occur in this position, joined in writing to the operator; for example, *he isn't coming, she mightn't be staying, they won't be needed*.
4. The operator is the item that is repeated in a tag question. Tag questions are 'tagged on' to a statement clause and request confirmation or disconfirmation of the statement. Examples: *he is coming, isn't he?*, *she hasn't been seen, has she?*, *they can't have been interviewed yet, can they?*.
5. The operator is the item in the verb phrase that is usually able to take contrastive stress; for example, *he IS coming, she HAS been seen, they CAN'T have been interviewed*.

If there is no auxiliary (modal, *be* or *have*) in the verb phrase in a clause that is a question, or is negated, or has a tag question, or in which the verb phrase carries contrastive stress, then the auxiliary verb *do* must be used. As an auxiliary, this is the sole use of *do*: to be there in instances where an auxiliary is needed but where one is not present (ie in case 2 to 5 listed above when there is no other operator). Following are examples based on the clause: *She likes cream cakes*:

2. *Does she like cream cakes?*, not 'Likes she cream cakes?'
3. *She doesn't like cream cakes*, not 'She likes not cream cakes'
4. *She likes cream cakes, doesn't she?*, not '. . ., likesn't she' or '. . ., likes she not'.
5. *She DOES like cream cakes*, rather than 'She LIKES cream cakes'.

It should be pointed out that the primary auxiliaries (*be*, *have*, *do*) may also be used as lexical verbs. Or, to put it another way, there are (at least) two verbs *be*, *have* and *do*: the auxiliary *be* etc and the lexical *be* etc. Here are examples of *be*, *have* and *do* used as lexical verbs:
Bert is an engineer, *She is having a lot of visitors*, *He is doing his homework*. Thus, if it is the last item in a verb phrase, *be*, *have* or *do* is a lexical verb; if it is followed by another verb in the same verb phrase it will be an auxiliary verb.

Non-finite verb phrases

All the verb phrases that we have considered so far have been **finite** verb phrases; that is, they have contained a finite form of the verb, showing tense distinction between 'past' and 'present', and being associated with a particular subject (first, second or third person, singular or plural). This function is performed by the operator or by the lexical verb if there is no auxiliary present. **Non-finite** verb phrases are those that consist of non-finite forms of the verb, ie the infinitive form (usually with *to*), the present participle, or the past participle, as for example in:

*I want **to go** home*, ***Going** along the road . . .*, ***Fixed up** with the necessary cash . . .* respectively. Present participle and infinitive non-finite verb phrases may also contain auxiliary verbs, but these must also be in a non-finite form (infinitive or participle). Modal verbs do not occur in non-finite verb phrases; they do not, in any case, have non-finite forms. The type (infinitive, present participle) of the non-finite verb phrase is indicated by the form of the first member. Thus a present participle non-finite verb phrase may contain a *have* auxiliary, as in *Having gone along the windy road . . .*; and it may contain alternatively or additionally a *be*-passive auxiliary, as in *Being encouraged by the crowd . . .*, *Having been asked about his identity . . ..* The infinitive verb phrase may contain a *be*-passive, eg *He wants to be fed*; it may alternatively contain a *be*-progressive, eg *They want to be going*; and it may contain a *have*-perfective, eg *He likes to have shaved before 8.00 am*. *Have* and *be*-passive appear to be able to combine in an infinitive verb phrase, eg *He regrets not to have been consulted*. This example also illustrates that a non-finite verb phrase is negated by positioning the *not* first in the phrase.

Tense

The grammatical category of tense is related to real-world time. Time is divided into past, present and future; and many languages have tenses marked in the verb phrase corresponding to these divisions. In English there is a clear distinction marked between past tense and present tense, eg *walk(s)—walked*, *show(s)—showed*. In fact it is the past tense that is marked, in its regular form by *-ed* (see further Chapter 18); and the present is marked only in the third person singular, by means of the *-s* ending.

The **past tense** forms of the verb phrase nearly always refer to actions and events in past time. But the reference of **present tense** forms is not nearly so straightforward. Simple present tense forms, eg *walk(s)*, *show(s)*, may be used for:

'eternal truths', eg *the earth is round*
habitual actions, eg *Bill jogs every evening*
present actions in a commentary, eg *Lilley comes in, bowls, and Boycott hits it for
  six*
future actions, eg *Harry flies to New York tomorrow.*

In the case of habitual actions and future actions the reference to 'habit' and
'future' is by means of the adverbial expressions, eg *every evening, tomorrow*; but
the form of the verb phrase used is present tense. Arguably, in a few uncommon
cases, a present tense verb may refer to an action or event in past time, eg *I hear
that you've had an accident*, where *hear* is a present tense form but presumably
refers to a past event. To refer to actions going on at the present moment in time, it
is usual to use a present progressive form of the verb (see below), eg *I am washing
my hair.*

What of the **future**? Clearly, a future tense is not marked in the verb in the way that
past tense is. It is generally thought, however, that the future tense in English is
formed by means of the (modal) auxiliary *shall/will* followed by the infinitive of the
lexical verb, eg *I shall/will come tomorrow*. But while this may be the most frequent
way of referring to future events, it is by no means the only way. In this sense there
is no future tense in English, merely a number of ways of referring to future time.
Among these ways are the following:

  shall/will + infinitive, eg *We shall/will visit the museum tomorrow*
  present progressive, eg *We are visiting the museum tomorrow*
  be going to + infinitive, cg *We are going to visit the museum tomorrow*
  simple present, eg *We visit the museum tomorrow*
  be to + infinitive, eg *We are to visit the museum tomorrow.*

As is evident from these examples, none of the ways of referring to the future does
so in a totally neutral manner: talking about the future inevitably involves talking at
the same time about intentions, plans, certainty and uncertainty.

Aspect

The grammatical category of aspect relates to the way in which the action or event
referred to by the lexical verb is regarded, particularly in respect of its extension in
time. In English there are two pairs of distinctions to be drawn: a verb phrase may
be regarded as either **progressive** or non-progressive, eg *I was walking—I walked*; a
verb phrase may be regarded as **perfective** or non-perfective, eg *I have walked—I
walked.*

The main meaning of the **progressive** in English is to view the action or event as
continuing over time or being in progress, rather than as just taking place. Clearly
some verbs are inherently durative in this sense, eg *sleep*, but even then the
progressive can be used and emphasises the progression or duration of the event, cf
*He was sleeping when the thunderstorm started, He slept while the thunderstorm
raged*. The past progressive, as used here, often refers to an action or event that is
in progress when something else happens. We have mentioned already that the

present progressive is the usual form for referring to events taking place at the present moment in time, perhaps because such events are viewed as spanning the present and including immediate past and immediate future, eg *What are you doing?—I am writing a letter*. One other meaning of the present progressive is to refer to a 'temporary' action or event in contrast to an 'habitual' one represented by the simple present. For example, *I water Bill's garden* refers to an habitual action, while *I am watering Bill's garden* (*while he's on holiday*) refers to an action with a limited duration.

The present **perfective** verb phrase (*I have seen*) contrasts with the simple past (*I saw*) in the following way: the simple past refers to an action or event that took place at some point in past time, usually explicitly referred to by a time adverbial or at least implied in the context; the present perfect, on the other hand, refers to an action or event which began in the past and which either lasted up to the present (moment of speaking) or has relevance for the present. For example, *I saw three kingfishers yesterday* views the action as taking place at that moment in past time, while *I have seen three kingfishers* implies that the speaker is on the look out for more, or at least that there is the possibility of seeing more. Compare also: *We have lived in Birmingham for ten years* and *We lived in Birmingham for ten years*, where the present perfect implies that *we* still live there, while the simple past implies that *we* no longer do. Compare: *I lost my umbrella yesterday in Oxford* and *I have lost my umbrella*, where the present perfect implies that the event is still relevant at the time of speaking—note that it would be impossible to add a point-of-time adverbial to the present perfect example ('I have lost my umbrella yesterday'). The past perfect (*I had seen*) transfers the meaning of the present perfect into the past, where it refers to an action or event beginning at a point in the past and continuing to another more recent point or event in the past, which has to be specified, eg *I had seen six kingfishers by the time dusk fell*. One further meaning of the present perfect is to refer to 'indefinite' past time, when a point in time is not or cannot be specified, eg *Have you* (*ever*) *visited Peking?—Yes I have been there* (*but I don't remember when*).

Mood

The grammatical category of **mood** relates to the attitude of the speaker or of the subject (of the clause) to the action or event referred to by the verb phrase together with the clause of which it is a part. Meanings associated with mood are realized in the verb phrase by the modal verbs (*can, may, shall, will, must*). On the one hand modal verbs realize meanings such as 'ability' (*He can swim*), 'permission' (*You may go now*), 'volition' (*They will look after your guinea-pig*), 'obligation'/ 'prohibition' (*The landlord shall be responsible for the condition of the premises*, '*You must not walk on the grass*). On the other hand, modal verbs realize meanings such as 'certainty', 'possibility', 'probability' and their opposites, eg *She may telephone us tonight, They can't have missed the train, That knock on the door will be the postman, She might have caught the later bus, They must have got home by now*.

The other use of the term 'mood' relates to clauses or sentences, more than to verb phrases, and refers to the distinction between **declarative**, **interrogative** and **imperative** clauses, illustrated by:

The secretary has opened the letters—declarative
Has the secretary opened the letters?—interrogative
Open the letters!—imperative.

These, too, relate in a broad sense to the attitude of the speaker, though perhaps more in regard to his interlocutor than to the action or event itself. This can be illustrated by the fact that the terms 'declarative', 'interrogative' and 'imperative' are not synonymous with the terms 'statement', 'question' and 'command' respectively. For example, it is possible to give a command using any of the moods indicated, cf *Open the window!*, *Would you mind opening the window?*, *I wonder if you would open the window*. As can be seen from these examples, the choice of mood reflects the relationship (or attitude) of the speaker to the addressee, and they could be regarded as constituting a scale of politeness or directness for commands.

Voice

The term 'voice' relates to the distinction in English between **active** and **passive**, a distinction that refers not just to the verb phrase (*I saw—I was seen*) but to the whole clause, involving a rearrangement of the elements in the clause besides a special form of the verb phrase; cf *The police arrested the thief—The thief was arrested by the police*. In an active clause the subject is the 'actor' or 'agent' involved in the action, while in a passive clause the subject is the 'patient' or 'goal' or 'affected participant' in the action. The passive is discussed further in Chapter 15.

Exercise 15
Analyze the verb phrases in the following, indicating for each auxiliary verb its type.
eg he has (perfective) been (passive) found (lexical past part); he must (modal) be (progressive) joking (lexical pres part); they might (modal) have (perfective) said (lexical past part)
 1. he may have sat
 2. he can't have been singing
 3. you have been drinking
 4. they are being stopped
 5. he doesn't know
 6. you wouldn't have been caught
 7. he can't have been being executed
 8. I haven't finished
 9. I might be seen
10. it has been being heated.

12. Phrases 3—Adjective phrases, adverb phrases, prepositional phrases

Adjective phrase

As the name suggests, adjective phrases have as their **heads** adjectives, eg *very enthusiastic about his latest idea*. As with noun phrases and verb phrases the head is the minimal form. From the example given it is clear that an adjective may be both pre-modified and post-modified. **Pre-modification** in an adjective phrase may only be by an adverb. Usually the adverb is one of a restricted set of 'intensifying' adverbs, eg *very*, *quite*, *somewhat*, *rather*, *extremely*, *fairly*, *highly*—which express varying degrees of intensity. Occasionally other adverbs may occur in this position, eg *beautifully cool*, *annoyingly simple*, *disgustingly rich*, *incredibly slow*.

The **post-modification** in an adjective phrase is sometimes called the 'complement' of the adjective. Three kinds of post-modifier or complement occur in adjective phrases: a prepositional phrase, eg *very anxious **about Jim's health***; an infinitive clause (clause introduced by an infinitive form of verb), eg *very anxious **to please everybody***; a *that*-clause (clause introduced by the conjunction *that*), eg *very anxious **that no-one should accuse him of laziness***. We have illustrated the three kinds of adjective complement with one head adjective (*anxious*), but adjectives vary in the kinds of complement that are possible after them. Many adjectives do not allow any kind of complement, eg *big*, *blue*, *astute*, *sudden*, *tall*. Some adjectives allow only one or two kinds of complement; eg *interesting* may take only an infinitive clause, as in *this book is interesting to read*; *attentive* allows only a prepositional phrase, as in *the audience was attentive to the speaker*; *safe* allows either a prepositional phrase or an infinitive clause (but not a *that*-clause), as in *this toy is safe for children*, *this tree is safe to climb up*. For most adjectives post-modification is optional; for a few, however, it is obligatory, the adjective does not occur without a complement; eg *aware* is always followed by a prepositional phrase introduced by *of*, as in *He was aware of a creaking noise*.

Adjective phrases have two uses or functions: an **attributive** function and a **predicative** function. The attributive function is when adjectives or adjective phrases are found in the pre-modification of a noun phrase, as for example in *a very interesting story*, *a somewhat anxious mother*. That is to say, strictly speaking, a pre-modifying adjective should in fact be regarded as an adjective phrase; though when, as is mostly the case, adjectives alone occur (ie the minimal form of an adjective phrase), it is more sensible from a practical analytical viewpoint to consider them like any other 'words' entering the pre-modification of a noun phrase. When an adjective (phrase) is functioning attributively, it may not, in any case, be followed by a complement. That is to say, adjective phrases containing complements (ie post-modification) may function only predicatively.

The predicative function of an adjective phrase is its occurrence after a 'copula' verb such as *be, seem, sound, feel*; for example, *Naomi is anxious about Jim's health, Jim seems concerned that Naomi will worry too much*. An adjective phrase functioning predicatively does not obligatorily contain a complement: as we have seen, some adjectives do not allow complements, eg *criminal* in *His actions were criminal*. However, we noted that some adjectives (eg *aware*) are obligatorily followed by a complement. This fact clearly implies that some adjectives must be restricted to functioning in predicative position (since attributive adjective phrases may not contain complements).

Indeed, an adjective does not have to be obligatorily post-modified to be restricted to predicative position. The vast majority of adjectives may function either attributively or predicatively, eg *the charming girl, the girl is charming*. But there is a small set restricted to predicative position, and likewise a small set restricted to attributive position. For example, *main* occurs only attributively, as in *the main reason*; it is not possible to say 'the reason is main'. Likewise *mere* is found only in attributive position, eg *a mere youth*, but not 'the youth is mere'. Adjectives restricted to predicative position include, for example, *faint* as in *he feels faint* (but not 'a faint man'), *asleep* as in *the dog is asleep* (but not 'the asleep dog'), and *alone* as in *the girl is alone* (but not 'the alone girl'). Some native speakers would include '*ill*' among this group; ie they would accept *the cow is ill* but not 'the ill cow'; other native speakers would accept the latter. Among adjectives restricted to predicative position and obligatorily followed by a complement are also: *averse* as in *I am not averse to a cup of tea*; *tantamount* as in *Her remarks were tantamount to slander*; *loath* as in *They are loath to leave this district*.

Adverb phrase

As the name implies, adverb phrases have as their heads adverbs. An adverb is the minimal form of an adverb phrase; indeed, many adverb phrases occur in the minimal form. An adverb may, however, be pre-modified; though post-modification is not found at all in adverb phrases. The only kind of pre-modifier occurring in adverb phrases is another adverb, usually of the same restricted set of 'intensifying' adverbs as is found in the pre-modification of adjective phrases, eg *very quickly, quite wonderfully', somewhat fleetingly, extremely faithfully*. However, as with adjectives, other adverbs may also function as pre-modifiers in adverb phrases, eg *amazingly well, understandably badly, horribly fast, incredibly gracefully*. This kind of modifying adverb appears to be either directly (*amazingly*) or indirectly (*horribly*) an expression of personal evaluation.

Adverb phrases have three uses or functions. Their main function is in the **adjunct** position in clause structure (see Chapter 13), to provide circumstantial information about the action, process or event talked about in the clause in which they occur. Circumstantial information includes information about the place, time, manner, etc of the action, process or event. The majority of adverb phrases have this adjunct function, eg *very soon* (time), *right here* (place), *extremely carefully* (manner), *rather noisily* (manner).

The other two functions of adverb phrases are the **conjunct** function and the **disjunct** function. The sets of adverbs or adverb phrases that may perform these functions are limited in number, and the adverbs involved are not, as a rule, modified. Adverb phrases with the conjunct function serve to link or 'conjoin' one clause or sentence to another. In the following example, *therefore* and *besides* are functioning as conjuncts: *Harry is inefficient. It is not, therefore, worth considering him for the post. Besides, George is the ideal man.* Other conjuncts include: *however, yet, moreover, thereupon, indeed* (see further Chapter 16). They typically come first in a sentence, or at least early on, and in writing are bounded by commas: *That, however, is another question*; *However, that is another question.*

Adverb phrases with a disjunct function also tend to occur initially in a sentence. The disjunct function refers to the expression of the speaker's stance or attitude to what he is saying; a disjunct adverb (phrase) reflects explicitly the way in which a speaker intends what he is about to say to be interpreted. Disjunct adverb phrases (unlike adjuncts) are not really constituents of the clauses that they introduce; eg *Frankly, I can't see George doing the job either.* Here, *frankly* is the disjunct adverb, expressing the speaker's intention as to how he wishes his statement to be understood; it could be considered a kind of abbreviation for something like *I am telling you frankly*, where *frankly* is now an adjunct of manner. Disjuncts involve the speaker reflecting on his own use of language. Adverb phrases functioning as disjuncts may occasionally contain a pre-modifier in the form of an 'intensifying' adverb, eg *Quite honestly, I don't see a solution to the problem.* Other adverbs having a disjunct function include: *seriously, candidly, bluntly, generally, personally.*

Prepositional phrase

Prepositional phrases are unlike any of the other types of phrase: they do not have a head, and thus also do not have a minimal form consisting of just one word. A prepositional phrase is composed of a preposition and a noun phrase, eg *in the garden, after the party*. Both elements are obligatory and neither may substitute for the phrase as a whole, in the way that a head noun may substitute for a noun phrase, for example. Phrases like noun phrases are said to be **endocentric,** while a prepositional phrase is **exocentric**. An endocentric construction may be substituted for as a whole by one of its constituent units; eg a noun may stand for a whole noun phrase, cf *big African lions roaming the jungle—lions*. In an exocentric construction no such substitution is possible, eg in a prepositional phrase both the preposition and the noun phrase must occur; one of them alone cannot stand for the whole phrase. Here are some further examples of prepositional phrases: *on the boat, behind the bus, on Friday night, into the final straight, at the stroke of ten.*

Prepositions are of various kinds; they have a relational role. The kinds of relation expressed most often are those of **space** and **time**, eg *beneath the spreading chestnut tree, throughout the long and stormy voyage*. Space may be subdivided into location and direction, eg *in the kitchen* (location), *towards the town* (direction). Time may be subdivided into point of time and extent of time, eg *before the wedding* (point), *for several days* (extent). A number of other relations are also expressed by prepositions; for example, **topic** as in *the chilling story **about** ghosts*; **purpose**, as in *a key **for** the opening of the safe*; **similarity**, as in *a boy **like** his father*; **instrument**, as in ***with** an axe*; **accompaniment**, as in ***with** a bowler hat*.

In all the cases mentioned in the previous paragraph, the preposition has a specific meaning, namely the meaning of the relation that it represents and refers to. Sometimes prepositions are used without specific meaning of this kind, when they are attached to particular verbs, adjectives or nouns. For example, the verb *blame* is followed either by the preposition *on* (*They blamed the mess on Jim*) or by the preposition *for* (*They blamed Jim for the mess*); in either case the preposition is predictable, and so lacking in specific meaning. Similarly, the adjective *interested* is followed by *in* (*I am interested in your offer*), and *proud* by *of* (*She is proud of her children*). The noun *anxiety* is followed by *about* (*There is great anxiety about his future*), and *sympathy* by *for* (*We have a lot of sympathy for you*). In all these cases the preposition has a purely syntactic relational function in relating a verb, adjective or noun to a following object or complement. It is more or less meaningless, since it cannot be replaced by any other preposition and thus enter into a meaningful contrast. Indeed, in the case of verbs like *blame on*, *blame for*, *wait for*, *look after*, the preposition is often considered to be part of the verb, and linguists speak of 'prepositional verbs' (see Chapter 11).

Given these two functions of prepositions, there are, then, two kinds of prepositional phrase. There are those prepositional phrases that represent circumstantial information about an action, process or event, indicating time, place, manner, reason, etc, and which have a similar semantic and syntactic function to adverbs and adverb phrases (filling adjunct position in clause structure). And there are those prepositional phrases which follow particular verbs and adjectives, and also occasionally nouns, as objects or complements. In the case of such nouns we are thinking of items like *anxiety about*, *desire for*, *submission to*, which require a specific preposition; rather than the more general post-modification of nouns by prepositional phrases (eg *the man behind the wall*, *the morning after the wedding*), where the prepositional phrase is functioning more like an adjunct than a complement. However, the post-modifying prepositional phrases here are providing circumstantial information, usually either of time or of place, about a 'thing' rather than about an action, process or event. Nouns requiring specific prepositions and complements are usually derived from verbs or adjectives, eg *anxiety* from *anxious*, *desire* from the verb *desire*, *submission* from *submit*.

Exercise 16
Identify the phrases in the following, and give an analysis in terms of the classes or subclasses of words that comprise them.
eg Understandably (adv P disjunct) Sam (NP) has declined (VP) the offer (NP); Sam (head N) has (aux perf) declined (lex V) the (ident) offer (head N). His arrival (NP) looks (VP) extremely unlikely (adj P) now (adv P adjunct); his (ident) arrival (head N), looks (lex V), extremely (intens adv) unlikely (head adj), now (head adv).
He (NP) could have told (VP) us (NP) this very good news (NP) yesterday (adv P adjunct); he (head pron), could (modal) have (aux perf) told (lex V), us (head pron), this (ident) very good (adj P) news (head N), yesterday (head adv); very (intens adv) good (head adj).
1. a very earnest look
2. he sounds very interested in our proposal

dis. 3. *adv.* unfortunately, [*NP.* he is very *Adj. Ph.* busy *Adj.* now]

dis. 4. a [quite *adv. Ph.* ridiculously worded *adj.* statement] — *NP.*

5. is he certain of our support

6. I am quite sure that he is certain to win

7. a rather baffling description

8. so, that makes it awkward to find

9. astonishingly, he can walk very fast

10. he was rather concerned that no-one should know immediately.

13. Clauses 1—Structure and types

The structure of clauses

Syntactic units are normally composed of units directly below them in the hierarchy, and they function in units directly above them. So a phrase is composed of words and functions in a **clause**; the word *the* is a definite article, which is a subclass of the word class 'identifier' and functions as a pre-modifier in a noun phrase. Clauses, then, are composed of phrases. And just as the description of phrases was in terms of the words and their function in various types of phrase, so the description of clauses is in terms of the kinds or categories of phrase and their function in different types of clause. The categories of phrase are those described in the previous three chapters, namely noun phrase, verb phrase, adjective phrase, adverb phrase, and prepositional phrase.

Function of phrases

There are five possible functions that phrases may fulfil in English clause structure: they are **subject, verb, object, complement**, and **adjunct** (abbreviated S,V,O,C,A). We shall now examine what kinds of function occur and which categories of phrase operate in each function. Other units besides phrases may sometimes operate in some of these functions; to a consideration of those we shall return later.

Subject

The **subject** function is normally filled by a noun phrase. The noun or pronoun that is head of the subject noun phrase is said to 'agree' with the verb in number. In practice, apart from the verb *be*, this applies only to the third person singular of the simple present tense. Compare the following: *The mice run up the clock, The mouse runs up the clock*; where *-s* is added in the case of the third person singular present tense form of the verb. In the case of the verb *be*, there are three forms in the present tense (*I am, he/she/it is, you/we/they are*) and two in the past tense (*I/he/she/it was, you/we/they were*). The subject normally precedes the verb in statement clauses in English; English is basically a subject-verb-object (SVO) language.

Verb

The **verb** function is always filled by a verb phrase; no other category of phrase ever operates in this function. It is virtually a defining characteristic of a clause that it contains a verb, either of a finite or a non-finite kind. Clauses without verbs do occasionally occur, but they may usually be regarded as derivations in some way from fuller clauses with verbs. For example, in the sentence *Dinner over, they went to bed, dinner over* could be considered to be a verbless clause; but it is presumably derived from *When dinner was over . . .* or from *Dinner being over . . .,* which do contain verbs. The most usual type of clause contains at least a subject and a verb (see clause types below). The common exceptions to this are **imperative** clauses eg *Get out*!, which are sometimes considered to have a *you* subject 'understood', and non-finite clauses eg *walking across the road . . .*, where the subject is 'recoverable' from the clause to which it is attached.

Object

The **object** function may be filled either by a noun phrase or by a prepositional phrase, as for example in: *Bill is expecting a big surprise, Bill is waiting for a big surprise.* In fact this second example may be analyzed in two ways: as we have implied, it may be regarded as being composed of a **subject**: noun phrase, **verb**: verb phrase, and **object**: prepositional phrase. Alternatively, the preposition may be regarded as belonging to the verb, ie the verb is *wait for*, a prepositional verb, and the object is then a noun phrase. However, it may sometimes be useful in analysis to assign the preposition in such cases to the object rather than the verb, especially if the preposition does not occur adjacent to the verb, as for example in *Mary blamed the poor result on adverse weather conditions.*

Some clauses have two objects, and a distinction is sometimes drawn between **direct** and **indirect objects**. The indirect object normally refers to a person, more particularly the person who is recipient or who benefits from the action. For example, in *Jim gave his wife a yellow flower, his wife* is indirect object and recipient, and the clause may be paraphrased *Jim gave a yellow flower to his wife.* In the clause *Agatha knitted her husband a yellow pullover, her husband* is indirect object and beneficiary, and the clause may be paraphrased *Agatha knitted a yellow pullover for her husband.* Sometimes the distinction between direct and indirect object is not easily drawn. For example, in the clauses *Jim sprayed blue paint on the kitchen wall* and *Jim sprayed the kitchen wall with blue paint*, it is difficult to determine which of *the kitchen wall* and *with blue paint* could be called indirect object. It is more satisfactory to talk in such cases of object 1 and object 2.

Complement

The **complement** function may be filled either by a noun phrase or by an adjective phrase eg *Jim has become a qualified engineer, Jim seems quite pleasant*, where *a qualified engineer* and *quite pleasant* are complements. What distinguishes a complement from an object? A complement has the 'same reference' as the subject, as in the examples given, or as the object when it follows this element, as in *I find Jim quite pleasant.* That is to say, the subject and complement, or object and complement, refer to the same person or thing, although without being identical or absolutely synonymous lexical items. This is not the case with subject and object, which are normally quite distinct in reference, unless the object is 'reflexive', as in

Jim has cut himself, or the object refers to a part of the subject, as in *Jim has cut his finger.*

As the previous paragraph implies, a complement may be either a subject complement (with same reference as the subject) or an object complement (with same reference as the object). Furthermore, a complement may refer either to a **state**, as in *Harry seems ill, I find Fred quite unpleasant,* or to a **result**, as in *Harry has become ill, That made Fred quite unpleasant.* There is a limited subclass of verbs that may be associated with complements; within that subclass one group takes a state complement, while another takes a result complement.

Adjunct

Adjuncts, which are normally optional elements in clause structure and may be freely added to any clause, give circumstantial information about the action or event that the clause refers to eg information about time (when or how long), about place (position or direction), about manner, cause and so on.

The **adjunct** function is filled by an adverb phrase, a prepositional phrase, or a noun phrase. For example, in *Tony walked there very quickly, there* and *very quickly* are adverb phrases functioning as adjunct; in *Sue walked to the farm after lunch, to the farm* and *after lunch* are prepositional phrases functioning as adjunct; and in *Liz walked ten miles that afternoon, ten miles* and *that afternoon* are noun phrases functioning as adjunct.

Obligatory and optional elements

When a subject, verb, object or complement occur in a clause, their presence is usually necessary to render the clause grammatical or sensible; for example, to leave the complement out of *Harry seems ill* would render it ungrammatical or senseless—'Harry seems'. Adjuncts, on the other hand, are usually optional elements: to leave the adjunct out of *Harry seemed ill yesterday* does not render the clause ungrammatical—*Harry seemed ill.* Subject, verb and complement are mostly obligatory; they must be present or the clause will be ungrammatical. Objects may sometimes be omitted, although some object is usually 'understood' when that is the case; eg in the clause *Jim is writing,* it is understood that Jim is writing something (eg a letter) or somewhere (eg in his notebook). Adjuncts may sometimes be obligatory; for example, in the clause *The waiter put the soup on the table,* the adjunct *on the table* cannot be omitted without rendering the clause ungrammatical—'The waiter put the soup'.

Exercise 17

Analyze the following clauses into phrases, indicating the function and category of each phrase.
eg The bowler (S:NP) threw (V:VP) the ball (O:NP) at the stumps (A:prep P).
The jury (S:NP) found (V:VP) the prisoner (O:NP) guilty (C: adj P).
The performance (S:NP) lasted (V:VP) three hours (A:NP) unfortunately (A: adv P)
1. The farmer was eating his lunch in the corn field.

2. The committee considers your proposals rather unworkable.
3. The transport manager could not decide on a new bus.
4. Jim passed the salt down the table.
5. The delinquent received a reprimand from the magistrate.
6. The milk has gone sour.
7. Gordon sent his apologies to the meeting.

Types of clause

On the basis of the functions of phrases occurring in clause structure, a number of basic clause types may be recognized. In English there are seven such basic clause types, which are specified only by the obligatory elements. They are:

1. Subject verb (SV)   *The dog laughed*
2. Subject verb adjunct (SVA)   *A policeman lives in that house*
3. Subject verb complement (SVC)   *That sounds a good idea*
4. Subject verb object (SVO)   *Everyone kicked the bucket*
5. Subject verb object adjunct   *The government sent the envoy*
   (SVOA)   *to Africa*
6. Subject verb object object   *They passed Aunty Ann the salt*
   (SVOO)
7. Subject verb object complement   *We imagined Uncle Bill much*
   (SVOC)   *fatter.*

Type 1 is an **intransitive** clause type. The verb refers to an action carried out by the subject that does not affect anybody or anything else. Also included in this group are the so-called 'impersonal' verbs eg *It's raining*, where the subject refers to a total environment rather than to some part of it.

Type 2 clauses may also be regarded as intransitive, although some linguists consider them to be more similar to Type 3. The verbs involved here take an obligatory adjunct. These are mainly adjuncts of place, either of position as in the example above, or of direction, as in *We went to the theatre*. But a few verbs take obligatory adjuncts of time or of manner eg *The performance lasted four hours, We live well*, where *four hours* is an adjunct noun phrase of time (how long) and *well* is an adjunct adverb phrase of manner.

Type 3 is the **intensive** clause type. The complement and subject are said to be in an intensive relation: subject and complement are not distinct entities but refer to the same 'thing'. An intensive relation also occurs when two noun phrases are in apposition eg *Mr Plod, the Policeman; That idiot, the fishmonger*.

Type 4 is a **transitive** clause type. For greater accuracy and to distinguish this clause type from Type 6, it is also called 'mono-transitive'. Transitive implies having an object, and monotransitive having only one object. This is probably the commonest clause type, both in terms of the number of verbs that enter it and in terms of frequency of occurrence in spoken and written language.

Type 5 is also a transitive clause type, but here with an obligatory adjunct in addition to an object. As in the case of Type 2, the majority of the adjuncts are of place, although other kinds of adjunct do occur. For example, in *They treated the prisoner badly, badly* is an obligatory adjunct of manner; and in *This car cost me £600, £600* is an adjunct of extent (how much).

Type 6 is the **di-transitive** clause type, ie having two objects. The two objects are sometimes distinguishable in terms of a direct object and an indirect object. The indirect object comes before the direct object and usually refers to an animate 'thing'. It may refer either to the recipient involved in the action, when the clause may be paraphrased by a subject—verb—direct object—*to*—indirect object structure, as for example the clause above: *They passed the salt to Aunty Ann*; or to the beneficiary of the action, when the clause is paraphrasable by a subject—verb —direct object—*for*—indirect object structure eg *They saved me a seat—They saved a seat for me.*

Type 7 is the **complex-transitive** clause type. There is in effect only one element following the verb, but it is a complex of an object and a complement. An intensive relation exists between the object and the complement, of the same kind as exists between the subject and the complement in Type 3.

In terms of the phrase functions making up clause structure, there are seven types of clause, but we have given only five labels to them, since Types 1 and 2 fall together under the 'intransitive' label, and Types 4 and 5 fall together under the 'transitive' label. There is no separate label to refer to clause types with obligatory adjuncts.

The constant elements in all the clause types are the subject and the verb. It is what comes after the verb that varies. What follows the verb is called the **complementation** of the verb; that is, the additional elements (phrases) which the verb requires for the clause in which it stands to be grammatical or sensible. Not every verb, therefore, may enter every clause type. Many verbs are restricted to just one clause type; for example, *seem* and *become* may enter only Type 3, *elect* only Type 7, *sit* only Type 2. Other verbs may enter more than one clause type, according to sense and context; for example, *find* may enter Types 4 and 7, *put* Types 5 and 7, *open* Types 1 and 4. Each verb may therefore be specified for the clause types it may enter, and in more detail still for the categories of phrase that may be associated with it in each clause type. This is part of the lexical description of a verb, and will be discussed further in Chapter 20.

Exercise 18

Analyze the following clauses in terms of their phrases, giving the function and category of each phrase. Indicate which clause type each belongs to, remembering that adjuncts may often be optional elements.
eg All of them (S:NP) called (V:VP) Harry (O:NP) a fine fellow (C:NP). Type 7.
They (S:NP) crammed (V:VP) the clothes (O:NP) into the case (A: prep P). Type 5.
We (S:NP) played (V:VP) snooker (O:NP) after dinner (A: prep P). Type 4.

1. The old fellow forgot about Jim yesterday.
2. I wouldn't make rice in that saucepan.
3. Your Madras curry smells appetizing.
4. You may not deposit your boots on top of mine.
5. They rolled the barrel into the courtyard.
6. You must not walk on the grass.

7. They consider poor old Andrei insane.
8. Barry sent Mary a bunch of carnations.
9. Your luggage weighs seventy kilos.
10. The children played in the garden all yesterday afternoon.

14. Clauses 2—Dependent clauses

Dependent clauses

In the previous chapter we considered the structure of clauses, ie simple sentences, in terms of the phrases that composed them. We shall now look at the other functions of clauses, that is, at clauses used other than as independent entities. We shall look, then, at dependent or subordinate clauses. We can distinguish three broad categories of dependent clause: **nominal clauses, relative clauses,** and **adverbial clauses.**

Nominal clauses

Nominal clauses, as the name suggests, function in the same places as noun phrases. We saw in the previous chapter that noun phrases function as subject of a clause, object of a clause, or complement of a clause. Additionally a noun phrase may function as an adjunct, but nominal clauses do not function in this position. There are four types of nominal clause, two finite and two non-finite. The two finite types are **that** clauses and **wh-** clauses, and the non-finite types are **infinitive** clauses and **participle** clauses, the latter usually involving a present participle rather than a past participle.

That clauses are so called because they are introduced by the conjunction *that*. They may function as either subject, object or complement, as in the following examples:
That Jim should take a bath amazed Penny (*that* clause as subject);
Jim believes that baths are harmful to the personality (*that* clause as object);
The possibility is that Jim is scared of water (*that* clause as complement).

When a *that* clause functions as subject, it is normally the case that a dummy *it* functions in subject position, and the *that* clause is **extraposed** eg in *It amazed Penny that Jim should take a bath*. Here the subject is the *that* clause, but it has been put after the rest of the clause (extraposed) and its position in the clause has been filled by *it*, whose only function is a place-holding one. English tends to consign long and weighty elements to the end of a clause, according to the principle of 'end-weight' (see further Chapter 15.)

Wh- clauses are those introduced by *who, what, when, where, how, why, whether, if.* They may be of two kinds, either an **indirect question** or a **nominal relative clause.** Indirect questions are relatable to direct questions eg *I wonder if Bill has posted the letter* may be related to *Has Bill posted the letter?*, *He told me what happened* is related to *What happened?*. A nominal relative clause may be paraphrased by *that which . . .* or *the place where . . .*, or by some similar phrase turning the *wh-* clause into a relative clause (see below) eg *What happened took Jim by surprise* may have the paraphrase *That which happened* . . . ., *Nobody knows where he went* is paraphrased by . . . *the place to which he went*.

Wh- clauses may function as subject, object or complement, as the following examples illustrate:
Where Penny had gone did not interest Jeff (*wh-* clause as subject), perhaps more commonly with extraposition—*It did not interest Jeff where Penny had gone*;
They don't know whether the bus has already gone (*wh-* clause as object);
The question is what we do now (*wh-* clause as complement).

In **infinitive** clauses the infinitive form of the verb may be of two kinds: either a *to*-infinitive or a 'bare' infinitive (ie infinitive without *to*), eg *I want you to go to the shops for me* has a *to*-infinitive, while *I saw him run down the road* has a 'bare' infinitive (*to go* and *run* respectively).

Infinitive clauses may function as both subject and complement, eg *To eat blackcurrant tart is to experience the ultimate culinary delight*, which illustrates both. But most commonly infinitive clauses function as object or as part of the object. Compare the following clauses:
I asked him to leave the room/I want him to leave the room. In the first of these clauses, the infinitive clause is functioning as direct object, while *him* functions as indirect object. It is possible to question both of these elements, eg *What did I ask him?, Who did I ask to leave the room*. The verb *want*, however, which occurs in the second clause, does not normally take two objects, and the questions applied to *ask* do not both fit; *Who do I want to leave the room* is all right, but 'What do I want him' is not possible, although *What do I want* is. This implies that this second clause is to be analyzed as subject—verb—object (rather than SVOO), and the object is to be regarded as a complex element made up of a noun phrase and an infinitive clause.

Participle clauses, in this case mainly with present participle, may function as both subject and complement; eg *Seeing is believing* which illustrates both functions; *Watching a wrestling match makes me doubt the idea of civilization*, where the subject is a participle clause. But, as in the case of the infinitive clauses, the most frequent function of a participle clause is as object or part of an object. In *Elephants like eating roasted peanuts* the participle clause is functioning as object. In *The keeper found the elephant munching peanuts* the participle clause is functioning as part of the object, like the infinitive clause in *I want him to leave the room*. Indeed, participle clauses never function like infinitive clauses in *I asked him to leave the room*, ie as a second object, unless they are introduced by a preposition. For example, with *They accused the keeper of giving the elephant peanuts* it is possible to question both objects: *Who did they accuse of giving the elephant peanuts?, What did they accuse the keeper of?*.

Exercise 19
Analyze the following clauses in terms of the phrases and dependent clauses that compose them, indicating for each constituent its function and its category:
eg Taking that bend at 60 mph (S: participle cl) explains (V:VP) how he left the road (O: wh-cl)

It (dummy) disturbs (V:VP) me (O:NP) to see so many people wasting their time (S: inf cl)

1. That people throw away money on gambling never ceases to amaze me.
2. I cannot imagine how the mistake could have happened.
3. He doesn't seem to suffer much.
4. You cannot order me to jump into the river.
5. I think that you will catch him stealing the apples.
6. They reported to the police what the prisoner had said.
7. It disappointed the candidate that few people came to hear him.
8. We do not know who will be his successor.

Relative clauses

Relative clauses function as post-modifiers in noun phrases eg *the old elephant which we saw yesterday*. They are linked to the head of the noun phrase by means of a relative pronoun.

The form of the relative pronoun is determined by two factors. Firstly, it is determined by whether the head noun (sometimes called the **antecedent** of the relative pronoun) is personal or non-personal. This factor basically determines the choice between *who* and *which*: *who* is used for antecedents that refer to persons, and *which* for antecedents referring to other than persons. Secondly, the form of the relative pronoun is determined by the function syntactically of the relative pronoun within the relative clause; for example, in *the man whom I visited yesterday*, *whom* has the function object in the relative clause; in *the elephant whose ear I tickled*, *whose* has the function genitive; in *the building to which I was referring*, *to which* has the function prepositional object.

Besides the relative pronouns already mentioned there is a further one, *that*, which may be used with both personal and non-personal antecedents eg *the singer that I like most, the song that I like most*. It is the only relative pronoun that may be used after *all, anything, everything*, eg *everything that I've said*, and after superlative forms of adjectives eg *the last example that I gave*.

Also used as relative pronouns are the words *when, where, why* etc, but obviously only after the appropriate head nouns eg *the time when food was cheap, the house where I was born, the reason why he kept quiet*. Such noun phrases are often reduced by omitting the head noun, in which case they become nominal relative clauses eg *when food was cheap, where I was born, why he kept quiet*.

Adverbial clauses

Adverbial clauses, like adverb phrases and prepositional phrases functioning as adjunct, give circumstantial information about an action or event, that is information about time, place, manner etc, eg *He always sings when he is in the bath, He always goes where he is not allowed to*.

Adverbial clauses are introduced by conjunctions which 'join' the adverbial clause to the main clause. The following are some further examples:
Conditional clauses, introduced by *if* or *unless*, eg *If it rains today, we won't play football, Unless you come early you won't get a seat;*

Comparison clauses, introduced by *than* or *as . . . as*, eg *Jane writes more neatly than Jim does, Jane sews as neatly as Jim writes;*
Reason clauses, introduced by *because* or *since*, eg *We can't go on holiday because we haven't any money, Since we have no money, we can't go on holiday;*
Contrast clauses, introduced by *though* or *although*, eg *Although Albert doesn't have any money he is still going on holiday;*
Purpose clauses, introduced by *so that*, eg *They've dug an air-raid shelter, so that they will be safe in the next war;*
Result clauses, introduced by *so . . . that*, eg *The pictures were so dusty that no-one could see what they were.*

In the same way that nominal clauses can be regarded as functioning as subject and object in clause structure, so too adverbial clauses may sometimes be considered as functioning as adjunct in clause structure. If this were always the case, the clause would be the highest or largest unit in clause structure, since if two clauses occurred together one would be regarded as functioning as an element within the other. But it is not at all clear that adverbial clauses may always be considered to be functioning as adjunct within another clause. For example, with conditional clauses it is not a case of adding circumstantial information about an action or event, but rather of setting two actions or events in relationship to each other: one is conditional on the other, and each event is represented by a separate clause.

Sentences

So we recognize a yet higher level than that of clause, that of **sentence**. Sentences, then, have a structure described in terms of clauses. And clauses may be related in two ways within sentences. They may be 'co-ordinated' by means of the co-ordinating conjunctions *and, but* and *or*, or by means of a conjunct adverb (eg *yet, so*), and here the relationship is a simple one of conjoining eg *Jim likes wallflowers, but Penny likes magnolias.* On the other hand, within a sentence one clause may be subordinated to another, giving the terms **main** and **subordinate** clause, or **independent** clause and **dependent** clause. Subordination is by means of a subordinating conjunction such as *since, if, so that, because* etc. And here it is not simply a case of conjoining but also of indicating a particular relationship, for example of condition, or contrast, or purpose.

Finally, a word must be said about the syntactic status of conjunctions. Conjunctions are words, but unlike other words they do not enter into the structure of phrases. Their function is to link clauses and so they function directly at the sentence level. In analysis, therefore, they are dealt with as separate items at the level of sentence (see the following two exercises).

Exercise 20
Analyze the following sentences in terms of clauses and phrases.

Figure 29: Examples of syntactic analysis

eg *If you like the book that he is talking about you should buy one.*

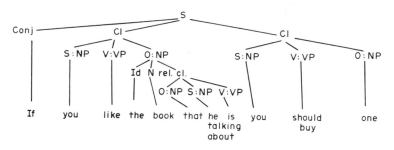

Barry likes to play football, but he doesn't often have the opportunity.

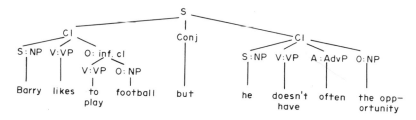

1. Although Jim finds the work difficult, he continues to do his best.
2. The politician that I admire most is the one who sticks to his principles.
3. Since elephants like peanuts, I am surprised that they haven't learned to crack nuts.
4. I do sometimes wonder if all this education doesn't drive people crazy.
5. If you do not believe me, you should look at the incidence of suicides among students.
6. The book about which I was speaking costs more than I would want to pay.
7. While he was deciding what he should do next, the tiger reappeared on the spot where he had been standing.
8. Penny considers that such pastimes are puerile, but Jeff enjoys engaging in them.

Summary

Now, as a summary of what we have been discussing since Chapter 8 there follows a review of the syntactic structure of English sentences.

In analyzing the structure of sentences we recognize a hierarchy of syntactic levels: sentence—clause—phrase—word. The normal relation between the levels is that units of one level function in the level next above and are composed of units from the level immediately below; eg phrases function in clauses and are composed of words. So to describe the structure of a unit at any level, we have to specify what types or categories of unit from the level below are involved and what function they are performing.

A sentence is composed of one or more clauses. A sentence composed of one clause is called a simple sentence, and its structure is the same as that of a clause. A sentence composed of more than one clause is called a complex sentence. In a complex sentence, either two clauses may be co-ordinated, or one may be subordinated to the other. In the first case two independent clauses are involved, in the second one independent and one dependent; eg *Jim came through the door and Bill went out of the window* (co-ordinated), *Because Jim came through the door, Bill went out of the window* (first clause subordinated to the second).

Dependent clauses sometimes function directly in sentences, as described above (conditional clauses, comparative clauses, concessive clauses etc), when they are introduced by subordinating conjunctions. Sometimes, however, they function directly in clause structure or in phrase structure eg *that* clauses, *wh-* clauses, infinitive clauses, relative clauses.

Clauses are composed of phrases. Phrases may function in five possible ways in clause structure: as subject, verb, object, complement, adjunct (SVOCA). As S may function: noun phrase, *that* clause, *wh-* clause, present participle (*-ing*) clause, infinitive clause. As V may function: verb phrase only. As O may function: noun phrase, prepositional phrase, *that* clause, *wh-* clause, *-ing* clause, infinitive clause. As C may function: noun phrase, adjective phrase, *that* clause, *wh-* clause. As A may function: adverb phrase, prepositional phrase, noun phrase, adverbial clause. O may sometimes be indirect object (Oi) or direct object (Od); as Oi may occur only: noun phrase, prepositional phrase with either *to* or *for*. O may sometimes be complex, ie noun phrase + *-ing* clause or infinitive clause.

Clauses may be divided into seven basic types, according to the obligatory elements that may occur with specified verbs: (1) intransitive SV, (2) intransitive SVA, (3) intensive SVC, (4) mono-transitive SVO, (5) mono-transitive SVOA, (6) di-transitive SVOO, (7) complex-transitive SVOC.

Phrases are composed of words. There are five kinds or categories of phrase: noun phrase (NP), verb phrase (VP), prepositional phrase (prep P), adjective phrase (adj P), adverb phrase (adv P)—each with a different structure. NP is composed of: pre-modification—head—post-modification. As pre-modification may function: pre-determiner—identifier or NP genitive—quantifier/numeral—adjective—noun modifier. More than one adjective or quantifier may occur, in which case there is a specific order within these groups of words. As post-modification may function: prepositional phrase, participle clause (*-ing* or *-ed* clause), relative clause, infinitive clause. As head may function: noun, pronoun, demonstrative, possessive. With all except noun there are restrictions on the modification that may occur.

VP is composed of: modifiers—head. As head may function a lexical verb only. As modifiers may function: auxiliary verbs, negative particle. Up to four auxiliary verbs may occur; the first one is called the operator. The negative particle (*not*) comes after the operator. Auxiliaries occur in the order: modal—*have* (perfective)—*be* (progressive)—*be* (passive). The operator inverts with the subject in polar questions, takes the negative particle immediately following, and is repeated in tag questions. If no other auxiliary is present, then for these operations *do* is the obligatory auxiliary.

Prep P is composed of a preposition and a noun phrase (the structure of which is described above). Adj P is composed of modifier and head. As head may function an adjective; as modifier may function an intensifying adverb. The adjective may be followed by a complement (post-modifier), which may be: Prep P, infinitive clause, *that* clause. Adv P is composed of a modifier and a head. As head may function an adverb, as modifier an intensifying adverb.

Words are divided into classes on the basis of common form, common function and common reference. It is possible to recognize nine word classes in English: noun, verb, adjective, adverb, numerals, determiner, pronoun, preposition, conjunction.

Nouns refer to 'things'. They are subdivided into proper (names of unique things) and common nouns, into mass (or uncountable) and countable nouns, and into concrete and abstract nouns.

Verbs refer to actions and events. They are subdivided into auxiliary and lexical verbs. Auxiliary verbs are subdivided into primary auxiliaries (*be, have, do*) and modal auxiliaries (*can, may, will, must* etc). Lexical verbs may be subdivided according to meaning or according to syntactic operation, ie which clause types they may enter.

Adjectives refer to 'qualities'. They are subdivided into attributive and predicative adjectives (most may be both), and into inherent and non-inherent adjectives.

Adverbs refer to circumstantial information (place, time, manner etc). They may be subdivided into intensifying and non-intensifying adverbs: the two groups do not overlap, and the group of intensifiers is a fairly small one.

Numerals are used for counting. They are subdivided into ordinals (*first*) and cardinals (*one*).

Determiners indicate the contextual status of a noun. They are subdivided into identifiers and quantifiers. Identifiers are further subdivided into: articles (definite and indefinite), demonstratives, possessives. Quantifiers refer to expressions of indefinite quantity. Determiners also includes the small group of pre-determiners (*all, both, half* etc).

Pronouns replace nouns. They are subdivided into: personal pronouns, possessive pronouns, demonstrative pronouns, relative pronouns, interrogative pronouns.

Prepositions are relational words. Sometimes they mean some specific relation, such as 'place at which', 'direction', 'time when', 'cause'. Other times they are simply relational syntactically especially after verbs, adjectives and nouns.

Conjunctions are also relational words, but they relate clauses rather than phrases. They usually mean something specific, eg 'time', 'condition', 'concession', 'reason'.

Exercise 21
Make a complete syntactic analysis, from sentence to word, of the following sentences:

Figure 30: Examples of complete syntactic analysis

eg *After visiting Milan they decided that they must see Naples.*

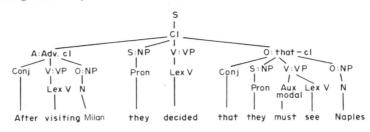

Although the patient seems much improved she will have to rest quietly for a few more days.

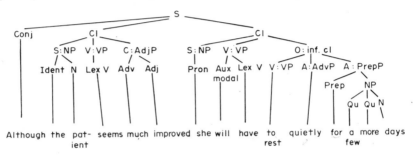

During the years that followed these three men found their destinies inextricably linked.

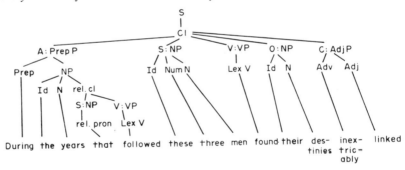

1. You must return that overdue book to the library tomorrow morning.
2. If the club secretary wishes to contact the opposing team, he should write a letter to the following address.
3. The grand old Duke of York had ten thousand men.
4. The small boy was quite sure that his father had told him that the earth was flat.
5. The old grey cat loved being swung through the air.
6. His younger daughter has grown very sullen lately.
7. You can tell me whether the 9·30 train has left yet.
8. The black pen that I accidentally left on the bus yesterday belonged to my uncle's sister.
9. However great may be his faults, he has achieved some notable successes in his lifetime.
10. After the snow shower had passed the weary travellers continued trudging through the deserted landscape.
11. It seems that the government is unaware of the difficulties which are being caused by its policies.
12. All the fifteen bomber planes of the squadron recrossed the channel safely that night.

15. Text 1—Rearranging items

So far all our considerations of the syntactic structure of English have been concerned with what happens within sentences, and more particularly within clauses. But we rarely speak or write in isolated clauses or sentences. Exceptions to this statement are perhaps signs and warnings eg *Keep off the grass, Danger, overhead cable.* Usually, however, whether in the interchange of conversation or in connected prose, a number of sentences occur. Sentences in sequence compose **texts**, and this term includes spoken sequences as well as written sequences of sentences.

Within texts sentences are not totally independent entities; they are connected in various ways with the sentences that adjoin and surround them. Textsyntax is concerned with the means of connection between sentences, usually between a sentence and what precedes, but also sometimes between a sentence and what follows. Quite obviously, we cannot account for the structure of texts in the same way that we described the structure of sentences or clauses, by isolating each element, in this case sentences, and giving it a function and a category label. The syntax of texts is not the same as the syntax of sentences: it is concerned with the ways in which sentences connect with each other, and not with the structure of texts as such.

Textsyntax is concerned with the description of two kinds of phenomenon. Firstly, it describes the way in which the elements of a sentence become rearranged in order to bring particular elements into positions of focus or prominence as demanded by the other sentences in its immediate context. And secondly, it describes the various devices that are used to link one sentence implicitly or explicitly with (usually) the preceding one: these are known as devices of **cohesion**. In this chapter we shall consider the ways in which sentence elements may be rearranged, and in the following chapter the cohesive devices operating in English.

Rearrangement of elements

There are a number of ways in which the basic order of elements in a sentence or clause (subject—verb—object etc) may be rearranged, and two principles of a textual nature influence such rearrangements. One of these is the principle of **end-focus**, which refers to the tendency in English to put new information towards the end of the sentence, which is a position of prominence: the nucleus of a tone-group falls on the last lexical item in a tone-group without contrastive intonation. Compare these two sentences: *I gave John a book/I gave the book to John.* Elements early in a sentence are usually 'given information'; they have been mentioned in the preceding text or context.

The other principle operating in the rearrangement of sentence elements is that of **end-weight**, which refers to the tendency in English to reserve the final parts of a clause or sentence for the weightier, more complex elements. We would be more likely to say *I gave it to the fat boy* than to say *I gave the fat boy it*.

Passive transformation

One common way of rearranging the elements in a sentence is to transform a basic **active** sentence into the **passive**; eg *Jim gave Mary a flower* becomes in the passive *Mary was given a flower by Jim* or *A flower was given to Mary by Jim*. The object of the active sentence becomes the subject of the passive sentence, so taking up first position, and the subject of the active sentence may be transformed into a *by-*phrase and take up final position in a passive sentence.

There are two principal reasons for choosing the passive form of a sentence, in preference to an active one. On the one hand, it enables the **agent** (= subject) to be put into the end-focus position; so that in answer to the question *Who won the battle of Waterloo?* it would be normal to say *The battle of Waterloo was won by Wellington*. On the other hand, the passive form of a sentence enables the agent to be omitted from the sentence altogether, either because the agent is not known or needs to be suppressed, or because there is no identifiable agent; eg *My favourite record has been damaged, Hundreds of people are killed on the road every year*.

Theme

We have said that the final position in a clause or sentence is one position of prominence (end-focus). The first position in a sentence is the other. What occurs initially is usually the **theme**, that is, what the sentence is about. In an ordinary active declarative clause, such as we have mostly been investigating, the theme is identical with the subject of the clause: the subject is the **unmarked** theme in an active declarative clause eg *The boy ate four apples*. In yes/no questions, the unmarked theme is the operator, eg. *Did you recognize Jim?*. In *wh-*questions it is the *wh-*word, eg *Who did you see?*. There are a number of ways of rearranging a clause so that the theme is **marked**, that is, an element not normally expected as theme for that particular kind of clause. This can be achieved by a simple inversion of elements, eg *Peanuts I like, but crisps I can't stand*, which has a direct object as theme in both clauses, or *Poor I may be, but I'm still happy*, which has a complement as theme in the first clause.

There are two special constructions for giving thematic and focal prominence to a particular element in the clause. One of these is the **cleft sentence**, which has the structure: *it—be—focus—relative clause*. *Jim found Penny last night in the casino* may have the following cleft sentences:
It was Penny that Jim found last night in the casino,
It was last night that Jim found Penny in the casino,
It was in the casino that Jim found Penny last night,
and *It was Jim who found Penny last night in the casino.*
The cleft construction is used particularly in written English, because it marks

unambiguously the focus of information. In speech this can usually be done by means of contrastive stress and intonation, but these cannot normally be represented in writing except by resorting to italicization, underlining and the like.

The other special construction for giving thematic and focal prominence is the **pseudo-cleft sentence**, which has the structure: Subject—verb—complement, where either the subject or the complement (more usually the subject) is a nominal relative clause; eg *What seems most likely is a good English compromise.* The subject represents the theme, and the complement is the element of focus. The verb may also be focussed in a pseudo-cleft sentence, which is not possible with a cleft construction eg *What he's doing is sharpening the knife.* The most usual kind of *wh*-clauses to occur are those introduced by *what*. Clauses with *who, when* and *where* are also found, but they are more likely to occur as complement than as subject; eg *The man in the bowler hat is who I mean, The Bavarian forest is where we often go.*

There is one further quite interesting transformation worth noting in connection with marked theme. In clauses with the structure: subject: nominal clause—*be*—complement (eg *To teach them is a pleasure*), which are normally realized as: *It*—*be*—complement—nominal clause (eg *it is a pleasure to teach them*), the object of the nominal clause may be taken out of the nominal clause and made the subject of the main clause, replacing *it*, eg *They are a pleasure to teach.*

The theme of a clause is usually 'given' information; it links with something that occurs in the preceding text or context. A subject noun phrase as theme typically has a definite identifier (eg *the*), which marks the noun phrase as 'already referred to'. Sometimes, however, the subject of a clause may be 'new' information, and it is inappropriate for it to occur as theme. What often happens, therefore, is that an 'empty' theme is substituted, and the new subject does not come initially. The most common empty theme is the so-called **existential 'there'** eg *There is a further point of view to be considered*, derived from *A further point of view is to be considered.* Existential sentences are derivable only from sentences that have an indefinite subject, and have a form of the verb *be* (either as a lexical verb or as an auxiliary) in their verb phrase; eg *Many fine pots have been discovered on this site* may be transformed into *There have been many fine pots discovered on this site.* In more formal or literary usage other verbs than *be* may occur, eg *There may come a time when England is ruled by a dictator.*

Postponement

Besides having means for bringing elements into thematic prominence, English also has means for transfering elements to the end of clauses and sentences, in accordance with the principles of end-focus and end-weight. These are called devices of **postponement**.

Perhaps the most important device of postponement is that of **extraposition**, when an element (usually a nominal clause) is placed at the end of a clause and its position in the clause is filled by a dummy or substitute element (normally *it*). The most common kind of extraposition is that of a clausal subject; eg *It amuses me to watch* *children playing their games*, derived from *To watch children playing their games amuses me; It doesn't matter what the result is*, derived from *What the result is doesn't matter*. Clausal objects may also be extraposed, and a dummy *it* replaces them too; eg *I find it amusing that children take their games so seriously*. Obviously the extraposition of a clausal object may take place only if there is an element in addition to the clausal object (complement, adjunct, or another object), after which the clausal object may be extraposed; eg *Jim owes it to Penny that he is always so neatly turned out*, where extraposition seems almost obligatory.

Another kind of postponement is that of a direct object in a clause with one of the following kinds of structure: subject—verb—object—complement; subject—verb—object—adjunct; subject—verb—direct object—indirect object. This happens if the direct object is particularly weighty or complex eg *They elected chairman the man who had worked all his life for the honour, They found in a mud hut all five of the lost children, Jim gave to Penny the last of the spring flowers*.

A further kind of postponement affects the postmodification of a noun phrase, If the postmodification is a clause, rather than a prepositional phrase, then it may be moved to the end of the clause; eg *The time has come to close the meeting, The eggs were bad that you sold me last week, They found the children in Cornwall who had disappeared the previous week*. Obviously in cases like the last example there has to be an unambiguous connection between the relative pronoun and the antecedent head noun. Noun phrases where the postmodification is postponed are said to be **discontinuous**.

Another kind of discontinuity involving postponement is that of comparative clauses, where postponement seems to be the norm, if not the only possibility. For example, *He has been less fortunate in his business deals than other entrepreneurs* is derived from *He has been less fortunate than other entrepreneurs in his business deals*, which also sounds acceptable. But 'More people than used to years ago own houses' seems to need transformation to *More people own houses than used to years ago*.

All the devices discussed in this chapter are means of rearranging the elements in clauses and sentences. The purpose of such rearrangements is often to sequence the information within a clause in a particular way. The need for such sequencing of information arises from the fact that sentences occur in texts; and for sentences to follow on from those that precede them, in terms of communicative content, certain elements need to be placed in certain positions. From the point of view of content, the clause can be viewed in general as starting out from the theme, which is usually given information linking to the previous context, and ending with the point of information focus, which is often the new information in that clause. These devices of rearrangement are particularly important in writing, where focussing cannot be achieved by means of stress and intonation.

Exercise 22

Consider ways of rearranging the elements in the following sentences.
eg Christopher Columbus discovered America.

America was discovered by Christopher Columbus.
It was America that Christopher Columbus discovered.
What Christopher Columbus did was discover America.

1. The old man sent his favourite grandson a wooden lorry for his first birthday.
2. I can't believe that Jim would do such a thing.
3. They found the man who had a scar on his cheek guilty.
4. Hundreds of elephants were gathering in the clearing.
5. Changing a car wheel is no easy task for a woman.

16. Text 2—Cohesion

Exercise 23

Fill in the gaps in the following text, where pronouns, determiners and other connecting devices have been omitted.

'It was dreadfully cold, snowing, and turning dark. It was __ last evening of the year, New Year's Eve. In __ cold and darkness walked a little girl. __ was poor and both __ head and feet were bare. Oh, __ had had a pair of slippers when __ left home; __ __ had been too big for __ __ in truth, __ had belonged to __ mother. __ little __ had lost __ while hurrying across __ street to get out of the way of two carriages that had been driving along awfully fast. __ __ __ slippers __ could not find, and __ __ had been snatched by a boy who, laughingly, shouted that __ would use __ as a cradle when __ had a child of __ own.

'__ __ little girl walked barefoot through __ streets. __ feet were swollen and red from __ cold. __ was carrying a little bundle of matches in __ hand __ had __ in __ apron pocket. No one had bought __ all day, __ given __ so much as a penny. Cold and hungry, __ walked through __ city; cowed by life __ poor thing!

'__ snowflakes fell on __ long yellow hair that curled so prettily at __ neck, __ to __ things __ never gave a thought. From every window of every house, light shone, __ __ could smell __ geese roasting all the way out in __ street. It was, __ __ , New Year's Eve; __ __ __ did think about.'

(from Hans Andersen, *The Little Match Girl*).

Most, if not all of the items left out of this text are predictable. They are often predictable from what has gone before eg the personal pronouns. Or they are predictable from the sequence of the content eg the conjunctions *and, but, after all.* They are predictable for the very reason that they reach back and join one sentence to another. They have a cohesive function, enabling the sentences in a text to hang together. Looked at from an alternative viewpoint it can be said that one sentence cannot be interpreted except by reference to another, usually the preceding one. For example, in *She was poor and both her head and feet were bare, she* and *her* require reference to *little girl* in the previous sentence for their interpretation.

Cohesion

Besides being about the way in which information within sentences is organized according to the demands of a text, textsyntax is also about the ways in which sentences are linked together into a cohesive whole. Five kinds of cohesion have been identified.* They are: **reference, substitution, ellipsis, conjunction, lexical cohesion**. We shall now look at each of these cohesive devices in turn.

Reference is defined by Halliday and Hasan as 'a semantic relation that ensures the continuity of meaning in a text'. It involves items that cannot be interpreted in their own right, but which make reference to something else for their interpretation. For example, in the nursery rhyme *Doctor Foster went to Gloucester in a shower of rain.*

He stepped in a puddle right up to his middle and never went there again, the items *he* and *his* in the second sentence are interpretable only by reference to *Doctor Foster* in the first, and the item *there* by reference back to *Gloucester*.

Reference in general may be of two kinds. **Exophoric** reference is reference outside the text to the situation; eg if someone says *It needs a coat of paint* and points to some object, then *it* has exophoric reference. **Endophoric** reference is reference to items within the text. It may be either **cataphoric**, ie forward pointing (eg *this* in *This is how he said it . . .*), or **anaphoric**, ie backward pointing, as in the nursery rhyme example in the previous paragraph. Only endophoric reference is cohesive, and in the majority of cases it is anaphoric.

Cohesive reference may be of three different kinds: personal, demonstrative and comparative.

Personal reference is by means of the personal pronouns, possessive pronouns (*mine, yours* etc) and possessive identifiers (*my, your* etc). The third person pronouns are nearly always cohesive, but the first and second person pronouns may often have exophoric reference. Sometimes a pronoun, especially *it*, will refer back not to a noun or a noun phrase, but to a longer stretch; eg *Curtsey while you're thinking what to say. It saves time. Alice wondered a little at this, but she was too much in awe of the Queen to disbelieve it*. Here the first *it* refers to the whole of the first sentence and the second *it* to the whole of the first two sentences, ie that curtseying while you're thinking what to say saves time.

Demonstrative reference involves the demonstratives (*this, that*), the definite article (*the*) and the adverbs *here, there, now* and *then*. All these are a form of verbal pointing and indicate proximity in text to the sentence in which they occur. In the case of the demonstratives, there is a tendency to use *this* to refer to something the speaker has said and *that* to what the other person has said. *This* and *that* may also be used like *it* to refer to extended text; in the example in the previous paragraph, the item *this* in the third sentence has this function.

Comparative reference may be either general, expressing the identity, similarity or difference between things, or particular, expressing a qualitative or quantitative comparison; eg *'I see nobody on the road,' said Alice. 'I only wish I had such eyes,' the king remarked . . ..*

Substitution is defined as 'a grammatical relation, where one linguistic item substitutes for a longer one'. The substitute item is therefore interpretable only by reference to the original longer item. There are three kinds of substitution: nominal, verbal, and clausal.

Nominal substitution involves the substitution of a noun as head of a noun phrase by *one* or *ones*, or the substitution of a whole noun phrase by *the same*; eg *My knife is too blunt. I must get a sharper one*; *Give me six currant buns. I'll have the same*. With *one* and *ones* there is always an element of contrast, and there is no referential identity. What is involved is different instances of an item, eg *These biscuits are stale. Get some fresh ones*.

Verbal substitution is by means of *do* (to be distinguished from the auxiliary *do*), and it substitutes for the lexical verb; eg *'Did you see Jim last week?'—'I did on Thursday'/'I might have **done**'*.

Clausal substitution is by means of *so*, for a positive clause and *not*, for a negative one. Here an entire clause is presupposed; eg *'Is there going to be a snow-fall?'—'They say so/not'; Are you going to the conference? If so, we could travel together.*

Ellipsis is similar to substitution, except that in the case of ellipsis the substitution is by nothing. An obvious structural gap occurs, which can only be filled by reference to a previous sentence. As with substitution, ellipsis may be nominal, verbal, or clausal.

Nominal ellipsis involves the omission of the head of a noun phrase, sometimes together with some modifiers; eg *Four other oysters followed them. And yet another four.; 'Which hat will you wear?'—'This is the nicest.'*

Verbal ellipsis involves the omission of the lexical verb from a verb phrase, and possibly an auxiliary or two, recoverable from a previous verb phrase. For example, if one were to hear the snippet of conversation, *It may or it may not*, one would know that it was elliptical, since there is no lexical verb. That would be recoverable from a previous utterance such as, *Is it going to rain today?*. Another kind of verbal ellipsis omits everything except the lexical verb; eg *'Has she been crying?'—'No, laughing'*.

Unlike clausal substitution, **clausal ellipsis** is not concerned with the ellipsis of whole clauses but with the ellipsis of large parts of clauses, whole phrases and upwards; eg *'Who was playing the piano?'—'Peter was'*. The whole verb phrase is not often left out in ellipsis across sentence boundaries, but it may be within sentences eg *Joan bought some roses, and Bill some carnations*. And it may be in conversation eg *'Where has Jim planted the roses?'—'In the front border'*.

Conjunction refers to specific devices (conjunctions) for linking one sentence to another eg *He was very uncomfortable. Nevertheless he fell fast asleep*. There are a number of words—conjunctions and adverbs—which fulfil this function. They may be divided into four groups: **additive, adversative, causal** and **temporal.**

Additive conjunctions simply add on a sentence as if it were additional information or an afterthought eg *and, furthermore, besides, incidentally, for instance, by contrast* etc.

Adversative conjuctions draw a contrast between the sentence they introduce or are contained in and the preceding sentence with which they form a cohesive relationship eg *yet, however, nevertheless, on the other hand, on the contrary, in any case* etc.

Causal conjunctions make a causal link between two sentences eg *hence, therefore, consequently, as a result, that being so, otherwise, in this respect* etc. And **temporal conjunctions** make a time link, usually of a sequential nature, between one sentence and another eg *then, after that, previously, thereupon, meanwhile, finally, from now on, up to now* etc.

Lexical cohesion refers to the use of the same, similar, or related words in successive sentences, so that later occurrences of such words refer back to and link up with previous occurrences. There are two broad types of lexical cohesion: **reiteration** and **collocation.**

Reiteration may be of four kinds. Firstly, the same word may be repeated in successive, though not necessarily contiguous sentences; eg *There was a large mushroom growing near her . . . She stretched herself up on tiptoe, and peeped over the edge of the mushroom.* Secondly, a synonym or near-synonym of a word may appear in a following sentence; eg *I turned to the ascent of the peak. The climb is perfectly easy*, where *ascent* and *climb* are synonyms. Thirdly, a word may be replaced in a following sentence by another which is semantically superordinate to it; eg *Henry's bought himself a new Jaguar. He practically lives in the car.* Here *Jaguar* is a term that is included in the term *car*, that is to say, *car* is a superordinate term to *Jaguar.* Fourthly, a word may be replaced in a following sentence by a 'general word' which describes a general class of objects; eg *'What shall I do with all this crockery?'—'Leave the stuff* there'. There are a number of these general words which have a cohesive function in texts. Referring to humans are: *people, person, man, woman, child, boy, girl.* Referring to non-human animates is: *creature.* Referring to inanimate concrete nouns are: *thing, object.* Referring to an inanimate concrete mass is: *stuff.* Referring to inanimate abstract nouns are: *business, matter, affair.* Referring to actions is: *move.* Referring to places is: *place.* And referring to facts are: *question, idea.*

The other kind of lexical cohesion is **collocation**. This refers to the habitual company which words keep. For example, the word *book* implies other words like *page, title, read, turn over, shelf, library* etc. A cohesion results, then, from the occurrence of a word's collocates, as well as from occurrences of itself, its synonyms or its superordinate terms.

This concludes our discussion of the devices that English uses in order to achieve unity and cohesiveness in texts. Without them texts would not strictly speaking be texts, but collections of more or less isolated sentences.

Note

* *See* Halliday, M A K, and R Hasan *Cohesion in English* Longman, 1976, on which this chapter heavily depends.

Exercise 24

Returning to the Hans Andersen text of Exercise 23, identify the various cohesive devices employed in the first paragraph.

Part Three: Words

17. Morphemes

In dealing with the structure of English sentences in the foregoing chapters we have taken words to be the smallest or minimal units of grammar. In a sense that is a true picture: syntax is concerned with the way that words pattern, via phrases and clauses, into sentences.

We have seen that above the level of the sentence we cannot speak of syntactic structure in the same way as below it. The same is true, though for different reasons, for structure below the level of word. Words do not have quite the same kind of structure as, say, a phrase or a clause. We have also noted that it is at the level of word that a connection can be made between grammatical items and phonological items. Grammatical words and phonological words are, however, distinct, because there is no one-to-one match between them; eg the phonological word /tu/ represents at least three distinct grammatical words, *to, too, two*. The distinction between the two hierarchies becomes more apparent when we go below the level of word. Words can be divided into syllables in phonology, but in grammar words are divided into **morphemes**. Any match between syllable and morpheme is fortuitous; many polysyllabic words are monomorphemic, eg *little, butter, carpet*.

Words, then, are analyzable in grammar into smaller units called morphemes. We are justified in dividing a word into morphemes if the units that we identify as morphemes can be recognized as parts of other words and have the same meaning or function. For example, *revitalized* can be analyzed into the following component morphemes: *re—vital—ize—d*. The unit *re* occurs in *retar, repossess, retake*, with the meaning 'again'. *Vital* occurs by itself as a word and in *vitality*, with the meaning 'life' or 'liveliness'. The unit *ize* occurs in *nationalize, pluralize, regularize*, with the function 'change this adjective into a verb'. And the unit *d* occurs in *tied, turned, loved* with the meaning 'past tense or past participle'. But it would not be legitimate to further analyze *vital* into 'vit—al', since, although *al* can be recognized in *national, communal*, it is not possible to recognize 'vit' as occurring elsewhere with the same meaning. It is irrelevant that we know that 'vit' derives ultimately from Latin *vita* meaning 'life'.

Exercise 25

Analyze the following words into their constituent morphemes, giving a meaning to each morpheme.

eg *preordained: pre-* before, *ordain, ed*—past tense/past participle *incapacitate: in*—not, *capacit(y), ate*—change noun to verb

1. undecided
2. devolution
3. fatality
4. impenetrability
5. reintroduction
6. makes
7. uninteresting
8. revengeful
9. wallflowers
10. disestablished

Kinds of morpheme

From the examples in this exercise it will be clear that a number of distinctions can be drawn between different kinds of morpheme. Some morphemes may stand alone as words in their own right, as well as enter into the structure of other words eg *vital, introduce, interest*. Other morphemes may occur only if they combine with another morpheme eg *re, d, tion*. The former are called **free** morphemes and the latter **bound** morphemes.

It will also be apparent that morphemes stand in a particular relationship to each other. In any word there appears to be one morpheme that is central (perhaps it could be termed the 'head') and one or more others that are peripheral (perhaps termed 'modifiers') and are attached to the central morpheme or to each other. For example, in *revitalized, vital* is clearly central and *re, ize* and *d* peripheral.

The central morpheme also often happens to be the free morpheme, which may be a word in its own right once the other morphemes have been stripped away. This central morpheme is called the **root**, and the peripheral morphemes are **affixes**.

Affixes coming before the root are called **prefixes**, and those coming after the root are **suffixes**. Affixes are always bound morphemes, and in English roots are nearly always free. A bound root occurs in, for example, *uncouth*, where *un* can be identified with the *un* of *undo, unsound, unwell*, but where 'couth' only occurs in combination with this prefix (compare also *disgruntled*). One further kind of affix occurs, sporadically, in the languages of the world, though not in English: this is the **infix**, which is a morpheme inserted into the root.

It is conventional to write bound morphemes with a hyphen on the side on which they are bound. So, *un* above should have been written *un-*, and *couth* as *-couth*; likewise *re-, -ize, -d* etc. Free morphemes are written without hyphens, since they need not be bound either side.

Besides being differentiated according to their position in the word, affixes are also differentiated according to their function. Affixes may function in two distinct ways: inflexionally, and derivationally.

Inflexional affixes, which are always suffixes in English, perform a grammatical function; they are representatives of grammatical categories. Suffixes in English that are inflexional include: plural of nouns eg *apple—s, pear—s*; genitive of nouns eg *man—'s, girl—'s*; third person singular present tense of verbs eg *walk—s, find—s*; past tense of verbs eg *flow—ed, play—ed*; present participle of verbs eg *go—ing, sing—ing*; past participle of verbs eg *create—d, show—n*; comparative and superlative degrees of adjectives eg *small—er, small—est, safe—r, safe—st*.

Derivational affixes, which may be prefixes or suffixes in English, have a lexical function; they create new words out of existing words or morphemes by their addition. Derivational affixes may be of two kinds: **class-changing** or **class-maintaining**. Class-changing derivational affixes change the word class of the word or morpheme to which they are attached. For example, *-al* added to *nation* makes an adjective out of a noun; *-ize* added to *national* makes a verb out of an adjective. Class-maintaining affixes do not change the word class of the word or morpheme to which they are attached. Derivational prefixes are usually class-maintaining eg *re—make, un—refined.*

There is not usually more than one prefix in a word in English, and from what was said in the previous paragraph it will be clear that prefixes are always derivational. There is never more than one inflexional suffix in English words, and it always comes last. A number of derivational suffixes may, however, occur. The relative order of morphemes in the English word is, then, as follows: prefix (derivational)—root—derivational suffixes—inflexional suffix.

Exercise 26
Give the morphemic structure of the following words, indicating whether the affixes are derivational or inflexional.
eg *impos(e) –ition*(D)—*s*(I)
re—(D) *attain —able*(D)

1. predetermined
2. reinterpreting
3. irresistible
4. inflammations
5. confidential
6. loganberries
7. unverbalized
8. deafened
9. hopefully
10. ironmongery

Analyzability

Not all words that appear analyzable in English are necessarily so. Sometimes it is possible to recognize and establish part of a word as a morpheme that occurs with the same meaning or function in other words, but not similarly for the remainder of the word. In such cases we are approaching the limits of the analyzability of words.

For example, in the following set of words we can recognize a derivational morpheme -*er* with the meaning 'actor' or 'doer' and which is used to derive nouns from verbs: *builder, runner, remover, player, butcher, grocer.* But if we analyze these words in this way, we are left, in the case of the last two, with the morphemes 'groc' and 'butch', which we cannot recognize as occurring elsewhere in the language as verbs. It is therefore not legitimate to analyze *butcher* and *grocer* into constituent morphemes, but we must regard them as unanalyzable wholes, in spite of their apparent similarity with other words.

A slightly different case arises with sets of words like *retain, detain, contain* and *receive, deceive, conceive,* where the prefixes *re-, de-* and perhaps *con-* may be associated with the same prefixes occurring elsewhere eg in *re-make, de-fuse, ?con-descend,* though not necessarily with quite the same meaning. But although the roots '-tain' and '-ceive' obviously occur in several words, it is not possible to assign any clear meaning to them, except perhaps by reference to their Latin etymology. So we either recognize such words as unanalyzable wholes or say that we are here dealing with bound roots that have unspecified meanings. In order to preserve the principle of the morpheme as a meaningful unit, the first solution is preferable.

Morphemes and morphs

We have spoken so far as if a morpheme is always composed of the same set of sounds or letters, although we have seen that this is sometimes not the case; eg *devolve* becomes *devolu* in *devolution, flame* becomes *flam* in *inflammations*. We need therefore to draw a distinction between a morpheme as a meaningful unit of grammar and the various phonological or orthographical shapes that it may be couched in.

The term morpheme is reserved for the unit of grammar and the term **morph** is used to refer to the phonological realization or manifestation of a morpheme. If a morpheme has more than one phonological realization it is said to have a number of **allomorphs**. These terms in morphology parallel the **phoneme—phone—allophone** terms of phonology. So, the morpheme *flame* has two allomorphs, /fleɪm/ and /fləm/, according to context.

Now consider the morpheme 'third person singular present tense' in the words *walks, runs, chases*. It will be apparent by comparing these forms with the first and second person form—*walk, run, chase*—that the 'third person singular present tense' morpheme has three allomorphs represented in these words, *viz* /-s/, /-z/, /-ɪz/. In this particular case the variation in the realizations of the morpheme can be accounted for in phonological terms: /-ɪz/ occurs after a sibilant as the final sound of the root, /-z/ occurs after other voiced sounds, and /-s/ occurs after other voiceless sounds. The allomorphs of this morpheme are said to be **phonologically conditioned**; their shape is determined by their phonological environment.

The allomorphs of *flame* could probably also be considered to be phonologically conditioned: /fleɪm/ occurs in a fully stressed syllable, while /fləm/ occurs in an unstressed syllable. But this is not the case with the allomorphs of *devolve*, namely /dɪvəʊlv/ and /divəlu/, although the alternation between /i/ and /ɪ/ and between /əʊ/ and /ə/ could be accounted for in the same way as for the allomorphs of *flame*. But as a whole the variation cannot be accounted for in phonological terms. We speak here of a **morphological conditioning**: it is merely its place in relation to other morphemes that accounts for the variation. So that we would say that the allomorph /dɪvəʊlv/ occurs when there is no other morpheme occurring, and the allomorph /divəlu/ occurs in combination with the morpheme *-tion*.

The majority of morphemes in English are probably realized by a single morph, but there is an important number, including most of the inflexional suffixes, which may have a number of allomorphs. We shall be considering these in the next chapter.

Exercise 27

For the following nouns of English, indicate in each case what the allomorph of the plural morpheme is:
eg *boat—boats*: suffix /**-s**/
goose—geese: vowel change /**u**/ to /**i**/

1. apple	apples
2. apricot	apricots
3. peach	peaches
4. sheep	sheep

  5. foot   feet
  6. man   men
  7. child   children
  8. tooth   teeth
  9. ox   oxen
10. calf   calves
11. bath   baths

18. English morphology

Plural morpheme

From Exercise 27 at the end of the previous chapter it will be clear that English nouns form their plurals in a number of ways. Some of the allomorphs can be accounted for by phonological conditioning. The 'regular' plurals can be accounted for in this way, with the same conditioning as for the 'third person singular present tense' morpheme, ie /-ɪz/ after a root-final sibilant, /-z/ after other voiced sounds and /-s/ after other voiceless sounds. This deals with the items *apples, apricots* and *peaches.*

In the case of *sheep* there is no identifiable allomorph of the plural morpheme. Yet we would say that there is a parallel equivalence between *The cow/sheep is grazing in the field* and *The cows/sheep are grazing in the field;* ie the first sentence is singular and the second plural in each case. It is convenient, therefore, to posit an allomorph of the plural morpheme to account for the second occurrence of *sheep* above, parallel with *cows.* It is usually said that the allomorph of 'plural' in this case is 'zero' /Ø/. So, *peach* + 'plural' is /piːtʃɪz/, while *sheep* + 'plural' is /ʃiːp/.

In the case of *foot/feet, man/men* and *tooth/teeth* we have another kind of difficulty in describing the allomorphs of the 'plural' morpheme. There is an obvious difference here between the singular and plural forms of the noun, but the allomorph of the 'plural' is not an identifiable segment of the word. If we say for example, that in the case of feet /fiːt/ the allomorph is /i/, then that implies that the root to which it is added is /f_t/. Now in all the cases we have so far considered, in particular the regular plurals, the plural allomorph is added to the singular form of the noun. The singular form of *feet* is *foot* /fʊt/. Does this mean that /ʊ/ is to be regarded as a morph realizing the morpheme 'singular'? But we have no such (allo) morph in the case of the regular nouns, and we should expect consistency in these matters. The solution is to revise our notion of a morph: a morph is to be considered not just as an element that is added to another morph, but also as possibly being a change in another morph. The allomorph of the 'plural' in the case of *feet* is, therefore, the vowel change from /ʊ/ to /i/ in the singular form of the noun; for *man/men* the vowel change is from /æ/ to /ɛ/ and for *tooth/ teeth* from /u/ to /i/.

In *oxen* there is an identifiable additive allomorph of the 'plural' morpheme, the almost sole surviving relic of a once regular allomorph of the 'plural', /-ən/. This is obviously a case of morphological conditioning: the allomorph /-ən/ of the 'plural' morpheme occurs with the morpheme *ox.* The /-ən/ suffix seems to occur also in *children,* but the situation here is more complex. What is added to *child* is, in fact, *ren* /-lən/; and there is also a vowel change in the root from /aɪ/ to /ɪ/. There are (at least) two possible ways of analyzing *children.* The first is to say that the allomorph of the 'plural' morpheme is both the vowel change and addition of the suffix, which is what is implied to the solution to this item in Exercise 27. The second analysis says that the allomorph of the 'plural' morpheme is /-ən/, by analogy with *oxen*, or /-lən/, and that the root itself has two allomorphs, one /tʃɪld(r)/ occurring before the 'plural' morpheme, and the other /tʃaɪld/ occurring elsewhere, ie in combination with no other morpheme or with a morpheme other than 'plural' (eg *childlike*).

This second solution to the analysis of *children* is probably neater and preferable. We have, in any case, to resort to the strategy of root or stem allomorphs when we deal with *calves* and *baths*. Here the allomorph of the 'plural' is perfectly regular, ie a phonologically conditioned /-z/, but the stem has allomorphs ending in a voiceless and voiced fricative for singular and plural respectively. That is, *calf* has two allomorphs: /kɑv/ occurs before a 'plural' morpheme, and /kɑf/ occurs elsewhere. Similarly for *bath*: /bɑð/ occurs before a 'plural' morpheme and /bɑθ/ elsewhere. This alternation happens with a number of nouns that in the singular form end in a labio-dental or interdental fricative but it is not a general rule; *cf wreath/wreaths*, where it does happen, *safe/safes* where it does not, and *cloth/cloths* where it may or may not happen.

The allomorphs of the 'plural' morpheme in English illustrate a number of the possible forms that morphs may take and the range of allomorphic variation that may occur. This variation has an historical explanation, which is, however, of no relevance to a synchronic linguistic description. The same is true of the 'past tense' and 'past participle' morphemes, which illustrate some similar problems to those of the 'plural' morpheme and some additional ones.

Past tense morphemes

Exercise 28

For each of the following English verbs, indicate what the allomorph of the 'past tense' morpheme is, and what the allomorph of the 'past participle' morpheme is:

		Past tense	*Past participle*
1.	save	saved	saved
2.	miss	missed	missed
3.	end	ended	ended
4.	hit	hit	hit
5.	fling	flung	flung
6.	find	found	found
7.	tear	tore	torn
8.	sink	sank	sunk
9.	run	ran	run
10.	send	sent	sent
11.	catch	caught	caught
12.	tell	told	told
13.	leave	left	left
14.	show	showed	shown
15.	do	did	done
16.	go	went	gone

In the foregoing exercise the first three items represent the 'regular' realization of the 'past tense' and 'past participle' morphemes. These allomorphs are phonologically conditioned as follows: the suffix /-ɪd/ occurs after root-final alveolar plosives, /-d/ occurs after other voiced sounds, and /-t/ occurs after other voiceless sounds. The 'past tense' and the 'past participle' have the same realizations. In the case of *hit* the allomorph is /Ø/ for both past tense and past participle. In the case of *fling*, *find* and *sink* the allomorphs are vowel changes. For *fling* the change is from /ɪ/ to /ʌ/, for *find* from /aɪ/ to /aʊ/ (identical for both morphemes); for *sink* the change is from /ɪ/ to /æ/ for the past tense *sank*, and from /ɪ/ to /ʌ/ for the past participle *sunk*.

In the case of *tear* the allomorph of the past tense is a vowel change, /ɛə/ to /ɔ/ *tore*, but in the past participle the allomorph is both a vowel change, which is the same as for the past tense, and the addition of a suffix /-n/ *torn*. For *run* the allomorph of the past tense is a vowel change, from /ʌ/ to /æ/ *ran*, but the allomorph of the past participle is /Ø/ *run*.

In the case of *send* the allomorphs of both past tense and past participle are the same, but of a kind that we have not met so far. It is not a case of change of vowel in the stem, but a change of consonant stem-finally, from /d/ to /t/ *sent*. With *catch* there is similarly a change of the final consonant of the stem, from /tʃ/ to /t/, but combined with a change of the root vowel, from /æ/ to /ɔ/ *caught*. In *tell* there are also two features of the allomorph of the past tense and past participle, a vowel change from /ɛ/ to /əʊ/ and the addition of the suffix /-d/ *told*, which is 'regular' after /l/. In the case of *leave* three features are associated with these allomorphs: a vowel change from /i/ to /ɛ/, a consonant change stem-finally from /v/ to /f/ and the addition of a suffix /-t/, again regular after /f/ *left*.

For *show* the allomorphs in each case are suffixes, but they are different: the past tense shows the regular phonologically conditioned allomorph /-d/ *showed*, but the past participle has the addition of the suffix /-n/ *shown*. The same is true of *do*, but here the suffixation is coupled with a vowel change, from /u/ to /ɪ/ in the case of past tense *did* and from /u/ to /ʌ/ in the case of the past participle *done*. The allomorph of the past participle form of *go* has to be analyzed similarly: a vowel change from /əʊ/ to /ɒ/, and the addition of the suffix /-n/ *gone*. But the past tense form of the verb *go* bears no phonological resemblance to the present tense form, from which past tense and past participle forms are derived (*went*). It is impossible to talk of the derivation of the past tense form of *go* from the present tense form, by means of suffixation or sound change. We talk in such cases of 'suppletion': a total incongruity in two grammatically related forms. All that we can state is that '*go* + past tense' = /wɛnt/.

Other inflexional morphemes

These inflexional morphemes in English ('plural', 'past tense', 'past participle') are useful to illustrate the range of variation that may occur in the phonological realization of morphemes. It is also an argument in the justification for separating phonology from grammar: it is clearly essential to have some constant grammatical notion of 'plural' or 'past tense' without having to refer directly to the phonological substance in which they are encoded. There are other, less variable, inflexional morphemes in English. The noun has a 'genitive' morpheme, as in *boy's* and *boys'*:

this morpheme has the same allomorphs as the regular 'plural' morpheme, ie phonologically conditioned by the final sound of the root. It will have been noted that the 'third person singular present tense' morpheme has the same set of allomorphs. A further inflexional suffix in the verb is the 'present participle' morpheme, which has only one phonological realization, /-ɪŋ/. The adjective often inflects for degree and has 'comparative' and 'superlative' morphemes, as in *quicker, quickest*: both these suffixes have the sole realizations /ə/ and /ɪst/. But these suffixes are interesting in another way, in that with some adjectives they do not occur but are replaced by the 'words' *more* and *most* coming before the adjective; that is to say, a word and a suffix seem here to be in allomorphic variation. With adjectives there is a small number of irregular cases involving suppletion eg *good—better—best, bad—worse—worst*.

Derivational morphology

Besides inflexions there is one further aspect of modern English word structure: **derivational morphology**. This branch of morphology aims to describe the formal relationships between lexical items and the ways in which new lexical items may be created from the stock of those existing. These relationships or processes are of three kinds: **affixation** (both prefixation and suffixation), **compounding** and **conversion**.

Affixation involves the addition of a bound morpheme to a root morpheme. In English, suffixation usually changes the class of a word, while prefixation nearly always maintains it. The following are examples of affixation: *internal—ize* (creating a verb from an adjective), *quick—ness* (making a noun from an adjective), *walk—er* (making a noun from a verb), *friend—ly* (making an adjective from a noun), *slow—ly* (making an adverb from an adjective), *anti—coagulant* (which remains a noun). Here also a morpheme may have a number of allomorphs, but not such complex patterns arise as with some inflexional morphemes. For example, the 'negative' prefix has the phonologically conditioned allomorphs /ɪm-/, /ɪn-/, /ɪŋ-/ (/ɪm-/ before root initial bilabial consonants, /ɪŋ-/ before initial velar consonants, and /ɪn-/ elsewhere), and the morphologically conditioned allomorph *un-*, which has a similar range of phonological variants, ie /ʌm-/ before bilabials, /ʌŋ-/ before velars, and /ʌn-/ before other sounds, eg *unpleasant, unkind, untouched*.

The process of **compounding** involves the combination of more than one root eg *star—gaze, witch—hunt, stop—light, waste—paper—basket, baby—sit*. In writing, these roots are either joined together or attached by means of a hyphen. The relations between the parts of a compound may be of various kinds; illustrated here are: noun + verb, noun + noun, verb + noun, adjective + noun + noun, noun + verb. And the resultant meanings are attained in a variety of ways; the examples have the following meaning relations: 'gaze at stars', 'hunt for a witch', 'light to indicate stopping', 'basket for containing paper that is waste', 'sit in and care for a baby while its parents are out'. For further examples of compounding see Exercise 29. Like other roots, compound roots may be subject to inflexion or further derivation by means of affixation eg *stargazer, babysitter, stoplights*.

Conversion involves no addition of new material to a lexical item but merely a change in word class. For example, the lexical item *net* may be both a noun and a verb; it seems likely that the object 'net', and so the noun, was the initial form and that the verb has been derived from it, ie by conversion. Similarly the lexical item *catch* is both verb and noun, but it seems likely that the verb is the primary form and the noun derived by conversion. Further examples are: *skin* (verb derived from noun), *push* (noun derived from verb), *invoice* (verb derived from noun), *win* (noun derived from verb). It is not always beyond doubt what the process of conversion is, eg in the case of *plan* which is both noun and verb.

This last type of process raises an interesting question of derivational morphology: are we dealing here with a **synchronic** or with **diachronic** (ie historical) matter? How these words came to be added to the language is a matter of history, and thus of little consequence to a description of how the language system operates at the present time, but there are two ways in which derivational morphology is of relevance to a synchronic study of the modern language. Firstly, it is clear that some words are related to others in form, differing only in the addition of some morpheme, and these relations are the proper study of synchronic linguistics. Secondly, many of the derivational processes that have brought new words into the language in the past are still **productive**, ie they continue to be used in creating new words at the present time. For example, the prefix *anti-* is still being added freely to all kinds of roots, as *anti-Common Market, anti-pornography*.

Exercise 29

Indicate the meaning relation between the parts of the following English compound words:
eg *sunlight*. light *given by* the sun
chessboard: board *for playing* chess *on*
flycatcher: *bird that* catches flies *for food*

1. daybreak	2. frostbite	3. driftwood
4. popcorn	5. handshake	6. brainwashing
7. matchmaker	8. mincemeat	9. drinking-water
10. typing-paper	11. sleepwalking	12. sunbather
13. homework	14. workbench	15. motorcycle
16. silkworm	17. sawdust	18. doorknob
19. tapemeasure	20. handyman	21. kettledrum
22. soapflake	23. cowshed	24. butterfingers
25. highbrow		

19. Dictionary information

Words

From our consideration of grammatical structures we have seen that words have a particularly important role to play. Sentences can be regarded ultimately as constructions out of words. And morphology is about the decomposition of words. Words are important from a further point of view: it is with words that we associate individual meanings. Words 'refer' to objects, actions, events, ideas, qualities in the world of experience outside of language. We can talk about the meaning of a word in a way that we cannot talk about the meaning of a phrase, or of a clause, or even of a sentence—although sentence meaning especially is important in its own right.

Lexicography

The aspect of linguistics that is concerned with the description of word meaning and interrelationships between words is 'lexis'. This comprises two related areas of interest: 'lexicography', the making of dictionaries; and 'lexicology', the more general study of words and the relations between them. In this chapter we shall consider dictionaries and the kinds of information contained in them, and in the remaining chapters some aspects of lexicology.

The lexicography of English has a long tradition on both sides of the Atlantic, a tradition which, until quite recently, has been more or less independent of the work and concerns of modern linguistics. The first dictionary to acknowledge the influence of modern linguistics was the American *Unabridged Webster's Third International Dictionary*, published in 1961; and here the influence was limited to the transcription system used to represent pronunciation, and to the abandonment of the prescriptive claims of the dictionary. *Webster's Third* claimed only to describe what people actually said, not to prescribe what they ought to say or how they ought to use words. More recently, dictionaries like the *Oxford Advanced Learner's Dictionary of Current English* (3rd edition 1974) and the *Longman Dictionary of Contemporary English* (1978) have been more widely influenced by modern linguistics, though these, especially the *OALD*, are intended primarily for advanced learners of English as a foreign language.

Dictionaries

Dictionaries fulfil two functions, which may be considered to be, at least partly, contradictory. On the one hand, a dictionary is part of the linguistic description of a language, that part which deals with the listing of the vocabulary (lexical items or lexemes) of a language and an indication of how these individual items fit into the general linguistic (syntactic and morphological) patterning of the language. On the other hand, a dictionary is a handbook for a particular group of users—schoolchildren, foreign learners, crossword puzzle enthusiasts, scrabble players, writers of all kinds—each with their particular set of demands and requirements of the dictionary. The first function demands a comprehensive list of the vocabulary of a language, or as comprehensive a list as the size of the dictionary will permit, including common everyday words which none of the users is ever likely to want to look up, eg *and*, *table*, *window*, *book*. A survey of dictionary usage among undergraduate students indicated that they used a dictionary almost exclusively either to check the spelling of words or to find out the meanings of words that were unfamiliar to them, presumably 'hard' and 'difficult' words. This would suggest that much of the information contained in current English dictionaries is not needed by their users.

Dictionary information

Let us now look in more detail at the kinds of information that are contained in dictionaries and what we mean by the lexicographic description of words. Let us note first that, as we have said, a dictionary contains, within the limits of its size, a comprehensive listing of the vocabulary of a language, including items common to the vocabulary of every native speaker as well as items more restricted in their usage. The items are arranged in alphabetical order, as a list of 'headwords'. In some dictionaries, derived words will not have a separate entry, but be included in the entry for the headword from which they are derived; eg *mysterious* will be found within the entry for *mystery*. Other dictionaries operate a stricter alphabetical sequencing, when *mysterious* will be a headword in its own right and come before *mystery* in the list.

Spelling

Clearly, a dictionary provides information on the **spelling** of words, by virtue of the fact that it is a written reference work; and the alphabetical listing facilitates the use of the dictionary for checking the spelling of words. One of the aims of Dr Samuel Johnson's dictionary of 1755, the first really comprehensive dictionary of English, was to fix the spellings of English words: he was by and large successful, our spellings today differ in only a few minor respects from those he laid down in his dictionary.

Pronunciation

Dictionaries also provide information on the **pronunciation** of words, usually by means of some phonetic script, often the International Phonetic Alphabet in most recent dictionaries, which is explained in the 'Guide to the Dictionary'. This is basically a phonemic transcription of the word spoken in isolation, since any variation due to the word's place in connected speech is part of the more general phonological description of the language. Some dictionaries indicate, additionally, stress assignment; and some give the syllabification of polysyllabic words.

Morphology

Next, dictionaries give information about the **morphology** of words, both inflexional and derivational. Usually, the inflexional information is restricted to irregular forms, since the regular inflexions are part of the general grammatical rules. But a dictionary would normally indicate, for example, that the plural of *foot* is *feet*, the past tense of *fight* is *fought*, the comparative of *bad* is *worse*; it would also give the pronunciation of these forms. As indicated earlier, derived words are often listed under the headword from which they are derived by affixation and possibly compounding; eg *fruity* and *fruitful* would be found as part of the entry for *fruit*, possibly along with *fruitcake*, *fruitknife* and *fruit salad*.

Syntax

Dictionaries give information about the **syntax** of words; that is, the way in which individual lexical items operate in the general syntactic patterns of the language. The amount of syntactic information given varies enormously from dictionary to dictionary. One way in which all dictionaries indicate syntactic operation is by giving a word class or part of speech label to every item. Designating an item as a 'noun', for example, indicates that the item may be used syntactically as head of a noun phrase, and so may be subject to the kinds of modification usually associated with nouns, or possibly as a noun modifier.

Designating an item as an 'adjective' indicates that it may be used either as head of an adjective phrase or as a modifier in the appropriate position in a noun phrase.

For some word classes the syntactic information in the dictionary may go beyond the simple word class label. It is conventional, for example, to designate verbs as 'transitive' or 'intransitive', ie to indicate whether they may be followed by an object or not, and implicitly whether the clauses in which they occur may be made passive or not. As we have seen, however—eg in Chapter 13—there is more to the syntax of clauses, and thus of verbs, than a simple division into transitive and intransitive would imply. Some of the more recent dictionaries, particularly those intended primarily for foreign learners, do give a more comprehensive indication of the syntactic operation of verbs, by setting up a number of clause patterns and indicating for each verb which of the clause patterns it may enter. Similarly, other word classes may allow a subtler syntactic subclassification; eg nouns into count and mass, adjectives into attributive and predicative, adverbs into intensifying and non-intensifying.

Definitions

Perhaps the central part of a dictionary entry for a lexical item is the **definition** or meaning designation. Certainly this is the chief piece of information that most people think of a dictionary as giving. If it is appropriate, a dictionary will divide the definition of a lexical item into a number of senses, which are related in meaning; eg *fatigue* has the senses*: (1) 'great tiredness', (2) 'the tendency of a metal to break as the result of repeated bending', (3) '(in the army) a job of cleaning or cooking'. If an item (a word form) has completely unrelated meanings, it is usual to assume the existence of two lexemes with the same form; eg *pupil*[1] means 'a child who is being taught', while *pupil*[2] means 'a small black round opening in the middle of the coloured part of the eye'.

Dictionaries usually define words by using other words. Sometimes dictionaries use illustrations, either photographs or line drawings (eg *Webster's Third, OALD, LDCE, Oxford Illustrated Dictionary*); and these are very appropriate for nouns referring to 'concrete' objects—animals, plants, buildings and their contents, machines, tools and the like. But that still leaves the majority of the vocabulary—abstract nouns, verbs, adjectives, and so on—to be defined by means of other words. Some dictionaries attempt encyclopaedic or scientific kinds of definitions of phenomena that are the province of science; eg the *Concise Oxford Dictionary* defines *wolf* as follows:

'Erect-eared, straight-tailed, harsh-furred, tawny-grey, wild, gregarious, carnivorous quadruped allied to dog, preying on sheep, etc or combining in packs to hunt larger animals.'

It is not always clear what dictionary definitions are attempting to do. In general, the principle operates that more difficult words are defined in terms of simpler ones—indeed, the *LDCE* limits itself to a basic 2000 word vocabulary in its definitions—but this usually means that simpler words have to be defined by more difficult ones, eg *fire* as 'the condition of burning; flames and great heat'.

Some definitions attempt to paint a 'word-picture'; eg *run*—'to move on one's legs at a speed faster than walking'. Others merely set one word in relation to another; eg *truth*—'that which is true; the true facts'. And others merely list words that are synonyms or antonyms; eg *altogether*—'completely; thoroughly'; *outside*[2]—'facing the OUTSIDE, opposite inside'. There is, then, no unitary form to the definitions of lexical items; the method depends on the word class of the item and on the nature of its reference. Here above all in linguistic description, language is turned in on itself, being both the object of description and the means of description.

Besides giving definitions, most dictionaries larger than pocket-size also give examples to illustrate the item or sense of the item in use. These examples are either composed by the dictionary compiler for illustrative purposes, or they are selected quotations from serious literature or from current quality journalism, or from some other collection of data, eg the LDCE uses many examples from the Survey of English Usage data.

Usage

Going beyond purely semantic information, a dictionary may give information about a lexical item's usage, especially if the usage is subject to some restriction or other. These usage labels are of three kinds: dialect, formality, and province. Dialect labels, such as 'American English', 'Scots', 'Northern' designate lexical items that are restricted in their geographical currency, or whose wider usage reflects an awareness of their geographical origin. Formality labels, such as 'slang', 'colloquial', 'informal', 'formal', designate lexical items that are restricted in their social currency, marking an item as appropriate to a particular defined social situation. Province labels, of which there may be a large number, such as 'music', 'anatomy', 'architecture', 'religion', 'shipbuilding', and so on, designate lexical items that are restricted to a particular profession, occupation or other area of human activity or knowledge. This section of dictionary information is as much part of the total linguistic decription of a lexical item and its operation in the language as syntactic information, and like this it frequently receives scant attention in published dictionaries.

Etymology

Finally, a dictionary, if it is following in the tradition set by the great nineteenth century *Oxford English Dictionary*, may contain information on the **etymology** of lexical items. Etymological information may include the origin of an item, the changes in its form during its history, cognate forms in related older languages, and possibly some indication of semantic change. Strictly speaking, such information is no part of a synchronic linguistic description: the origin of forms, while useful for those interested in the history of the language, does not contribute directly to the knowledge of the way in which the language operates at the present time.

Summarizing, we have said that dictionaries, if they are to be part of the synchronic lexical description of a language, should contain in their entries the following information: orthographical (spelling), phonological (pronunciation, including stress and syllabification), morphological (irregular inflexions, and derivations), syntactic (giving a precise description of the operation of individual items), semantic (definitions of all senses distinguished, together with illustrative examples), stylistic (restricted usage of a geographical, social and occupational kind).

Here now is a sample entry for the verbs *believe* and *sew*, based on the *Longman Dictionary of Contemporary English* entries:

believe /bɔˈliːv/ v
(1) S V 'to have a firm religious faith'
(2) S V O:NP 'to consider to be true or honest'—*to believe someone, to believe someone's reports*
· (3) S V O: *that*-cl, NP + inf-cl; S V O:NP (to be) C
    'to hold as an opinion; suppose'—*I believe (that) he has come,*
    I believe him to have done it, I believe him (to be) honest
believable /bɔˈliːvəbəl/ adj
'that can be believed'
believer /bɔˈliːvəʳ/ n
'person who has (religious) faith'

sew /səʊ/ v past tense **sewed** /səʊd/, past part **sewn** /səʊn/
(1) S V; S V O:NP 'to join or fasten (cloth, leather, paper, etc) by stitches made with thread; make or mend (esp. pieces of clothing) with needle and thread'—*Would you sew on this button/sew this button onto my shirt?*
(2) S V O:NP A:PrepP 'to enclose in this way'—*She sewed a £5 note inside/into his pocket*
sewer /ˈsəʊə/ n 'person who sews'
sewing /ˈsəʊɪŋ/ n 'the act of sewing', 'work made in this way'.

Exercise 30
Write dictionary entries on the pattern given for the verbs *bake* and *mislead*.

Note

* Definitions quoted here and following are from or adapted from those in the *Longman Dictionary of Contemporary English*.

20. 'Grammar' of words

'The fills basined the apply out of the squeeze' It is clear that a word may not combine freely with just any other word or words: there are constraints on the 'grammar' or combinability of words. Some constraints arise from the general grammatical or syntactic system of the language, from the rules for phrase, clause and sentence structure. Other constraints arise from the nature of the word itself and its particular place and function in the language as a whole. The first kind of constraint can be illustrated by the fact that adjectives usually precede nouns in noun phrases, or that subject noun phrases usually precede verb phrases in the structure of declarative clauses. Constraints of the second kind fall into two categories. On the one hand there are constraints which are purely syntactic, arising from the classification and subclassification of the word. On the other hand there are constraints which are more of a semantic nature, 'collocational' restraints. We will now look at these categories of constraint in more detail.

Syntactic constraints

As may be seen by looking at dictionary entries, the word class label of a word (noun, verb, preposition, etc) is a designation of the syntactic operation of a word. So, the label 'noun' indicates in a fairly specific way where in syntactic structure a word with that label may operate, ie as head of a noun phrase, as a modifier immediately before the head in a noun phrase. The label 'adjective' indicates that the word so labelled may operate as head of an adjective phrase, or as modifier after a determiner and before a noun modifier in a noun phrase. But in general these broad word class labels are not in themselves sufficient to specify all the constraints operating for individual items in the class: they refer to the class as a whole. Not all nouns, for example, may operate as noun modifiers. There is therefore a need to subclassify, particularly in the open classes.

In the case of nouns, then, a subclassification needs to be made into those that may function as modifiers in noun phrases and those that may not. Again in the case of nouns, a number of compatibilities with determiners need to be accounted for. This will entail a subclassification into count nouns and mass nouns, the latter being compatible with a 'Ø' determiner, *some* and *the*, and the former being compatible with 'Ø', *a, the, some, many* etc (compare *butter* and *saucepan*). Furthermore, some nouns may be followed by particular post-modifiers; for example, *determination* may be followed by a *to*-infinitive clause (*his determination to succeed*); *affection* by a prepositional phrase introduced by *for* (*his affection for Lucy*); *regret* by a *that*-clause (*his regret that he had failed*). This syntactic constraint also needs to be accounted for by subclassification.

In the case of verbs, a basic distinction needs to be made between those which function as the head of a verb phrase, ie lexical verbs, and those which have an auxiliary function. Auxiliary verbs need to be further subclassified into primary auxiliaries and modal auxiliaries, and according to the position they may occupy in the verb phrase. Lexical verbs, on the other hand, have to be subclassified according to the types of structure in which they may occur. Basically this involves the kinds of object, complement and obligatory adjunct that may co-occur with a particular verb, sometimes called the 'complementation' of the verb. For example, there will be a subclass of verbs like *remember*, which enter a 'SVO' structure, where the object may be a noun phrase (*Do you remember Jim*), a *that*-clause (*He remembered that he was supposed to phone her*), a *to*-infinitive clause (*He remembered to phone her*), or a *wh*-clause (*Do you remember where I hid the key?*); and which also enter a 'SVOC' structure, where the object is a noun phrase and the complement is an adjective phrase (*I remember him bald*) or a noun phrase (*I remember him a young man*).

This kind of subclassification obviously goes much further than the traditional distinction between 'transitive' and 'intransitive'. However, this latter distinction is important from another point of view: part of the lexical information about a verb is its ability or otherwise to be made passive, or more accurately for the clause in which it occurs to be made passive, and the transitive-intransitive distinction represents this information. Transitive verbs are those taking objects, ie entering mono-transitive, di-transitive and complex-transitive structures, and this is a pre-requisite for the passive transformation. The notion may have to be broadened, however, to take account of the fact that some prepositional phrases functioning as adjunct may become the subject of a passive clause eg *My chair has been sat on*.

We have seen that to take account of the syntax of adjectives a subclassification into attributive adjectives and predicative adjectives is required, since some adjectives are restricted to one or the other of these two positions, eg *mere* to the attributive position (*a mere boy*), and *asleep* to the predicative position (*the boy is asleep*). A subclassification of adjectives also needs to be made in order to distinguish between those adjectives which may take complements and those which may not, and to indicate which kinds of complement are involved in each case. For example, *ready* may be followed by a *to*-infinitive clause (*they are ready to admit defeat*) or a prepositional phrase (*they are ready for their meal*); *sorry* may be followed by a to-infinitive clause (*I am sorry to call at this hour*), a *that*-clause (*I am sorry that you are disappointed*) or a prepositional phrase introduced by *for* or *about* (*I am sorry for Jim, about the mess*).

Adverbs, as we discussed earlier, are subclassified into intensifying and non-intensifying, the latter functioning as head in an adverb phrase and the former as modifier in an adverb phrase or an adjective phrase. One group of adverbs presents an interesting problem of classification. Compare the status of *off* in the following clauses: *Jim jumped off the bus; Jim jumped off.* The first of these clauses would be analyzed as: S:NP V:VP A:prep P, ie *off* would be classed as a preposition. The second clause would be analyzed as: S:NP V:VP A:adv P, ie *off* would be classed as an adverb. But consider *The meeting is off*, where *off* would again be classed as an adverb. But this case is different from *Jim jumped off*, since here *off* could not be completed with a noun phrase to become a prepositional phrase. In other words, in *Jim jumped off* the word *off* appears to be both adverb and at least potentially preposition. We can either assign *off* to both the class of prepositions and the class of adverbs, or we can create a new class of words, adverb-prepositions, which would include those which function like *off*, but not like *to* (a preposition only), nor like *away* (an adverb only).

Collocational restraints

This, then, is one kind of constraint on the combinability of words, a syntactic one. Now let us turn to the collocational constraints on word combinations. 'Collocation' is a term that has been used in a number of ways. We shall use it to refer to two kinds of combinability: firstly, the regular expectations that a word has for one or more other words; and secondly, the semantic compatibilities that exist between words having particular syntactic functions.

The first sense of collocation covers facts like the following: in geometry we say that we *describe a circle, construct a triangle* and *drop a perpendicular*, where all these verbs refer to drawing a particular line or series of lines on a two-dimensional surface. But these kinds of compatibility are not restricted to specialized registers. We talk of someone *raising* his eyebrows, not *lifting* them. We talk of a *powerful* motorcar, but of *strong* coffee, and of both *powerful* and *strong* arguments. We talk of *raising* or *breeding* cattle, but of *bringing up* children (though *raise* is perhaps possible here also), and of *breeding* dogs or cats. Compare also the collocations of *good, strong* and *high* with the nouns *likelihood, probability, possibility* and *chance*:[1]

good likelihood	strong likelihood	high
	probability	probability
possibility	possibility	
chance		

From this notion of collocation derives the idea that some words have a strong mutual expectancy, eg *lay* and *egg, knead* and *dough, white* or *black* and *coffee, turn on* or *turn off* and *switch* or *tap*. Obviously many of these expectancies arise from the extra-linguistic situation that the words are referring to; we are after all dealing here with semantic constraints. When the expectancies become particularly strong, and words are continually found in each others' company, then this gives rise to the development of idioms and clichés. For example, the following would count as idioms: *red revolution, purple passage, be worth while, find fault with, seek help from, to and fro, kith and kin, without let or hindrance*; and the following as clichés: *desirable residence* in estate agents' blurb, *at this present moment in time* in politicians' speeches, *exclusive interview* or *revelation* in journalistic jargon, *unrepeatable offer* in salesmen's talk, and perhaps *real meaning* in students' essays!

The other sense of collocation, referring to the semantic compatibilities between words having a particular syntactic function, may be illustrated by a sentence that has become a classic in linguistics: *Colourless green ideas sleep furiously*[2]. *Colourless* and *green* are semantically incompatible adjectives; they in turn are incompatible with the noun *idea*, since ideas cannot have colour predicated of them.

Likewise *idea* is incompatible with *sleep*, since that is not something that ideas are deemed capable of doing; and *sleep* is incompatible with the adverb *furiously*, since that is not a way in which people can sleep. Obviously, these incompatibilities arise from the nature of extra-linguistic reality; but it is nevertheless arguable that they reflect facts about the operation of words in the language system, facts that need to be taken account of in a linguistic description.

We have so far stated the matter rather negatively, in terms of incompatibilities. It is possible to make more positive statements. For example, taking the verb *eat*, it is possible to say of this verb that the subject associated with it must be a noun phrase referring to an animate object, human or animal, and that the object must refer to an edible object, food, meat, cereal, plants etc. By stating the regular collocations of words in this way it is possible to account quite easily for metaphor. For example, the sentence *He ate his words* will obviously be classed as metaphorical, since words are not normally edible objects. As in the case of syntactic compatibilities, it is easier to state semantic collocational compatibilities in terms of what particular verbs require, rather than in terms of what particular nouns require. For example, the noun *man* as subject could require any of the verbs that refer to actions that men are capable of doing. This merely emphasizes the centrality of the verb in the clause, and its function as the departure point in description, if not in communication.

As a postscript, let us come back to the question of what is a word. We have distinguished between phonological, grammatical and lexical words (also called **lexical items** or **lexemes**). Given the notion of collocation, and more especially the notion of idiom or fixed collocation, it seems that we shall have to recognize as lexical items groups of more than one word, in an orthographic sense, and consider them to have the same value in the language system as individual words. For example, in the clause *She went at him hammer and tongs*, the last three words constitute a single lexical item. This can be demonstrated if we consider its syntactic status, ie whether it should be classed as a noun or as an adverb. Using the criterion of word classification that we have already established, namely that of function, we see that *hammer and tongs* here functions as head of an adverb phrase functioning as adjunct in the clause and referring to the 'manner' of the action. Since it is head of an adverb phrase it must be considered to be an adverb, even though analytically the individual parts are nouns. In other words, our principles of classification will on occasions compel us to regard groups of orthographic words as single lexical items from a structural point of view.

Notes

[1] From Bolinger, D *Aspects of language* Harcourt Brace Jovanovich 2nd edn, 1975. p. 103.
[2] Coined by Noam Chomsky in *Syntactic structures* Mouton, 1957. p. 15.

Exercise 31

Work out the semantic compatibilities of the following verbs:
eg *howl*: Subject animal, eg wolf
mend: Subject human, object broken thing

1. admire	2. bark	3. laugh
4. prove	5. trot	6. sail
7. spoil	8. weep.	

21. Relations between words

In the previous chapter we looked at the syntax and collocation of lexical items, that is the relations between words on the **syntagmatic level**, the ability of words to combine. We may also consider the relations between words from the **paradigmatic** point of view, how words relate to each other hierarchically or as substitutes for one another. We shall consider three kinds of paradigmatic relation among words: the attempt to identify 'semantic features', the relations of 'sense', and the attempt to organize vocabulary into lexical or semantic 'fields'.

Semantic features

The identification of **semantic features** is an attempt to relate lexical items by decomposing meanings into 'features' that recur in the meanings of several lexical items. These features tend to be universal categories of meaning, reflecting the nature of the universe in which we live. One such feature is CONCRETE (features are conventionally written with capital letters), which serves to distinguish words like *dog, plant* and *stone* from words like *truth, joy* and *ability*. The latter are often called 'abstract' nouns; but in feature analysis it is usual for each feature to represent a binary choice. So the first set of words would be called +CONCRETE, and the second set −CONCRETE. Words that have the feature +CONCRETE may be further differentiated by the feature ORGANIC, which distinguishes *dog* and *plant* from *stone* and *table*, the former being +ORGANIC and the latter −ORGANIC. Words that have the feature +ORGANIC may be further differentiated by means of the feature ANIMATE: *plant* is −ANIMATE, while *dog* is +ANIMATE. And +ANIMATE words may be further differentiated by the feature HUMAN: *dog* is −HUMAN, while *boy* is +HUMAN. The features associated with *boy* are, then, +HUMAN, +ANIMATE, +ORGANIC, +CONCRETE.

Considered like this, the features appear to be hierarchically ordered:

Figure 31: Semantic features

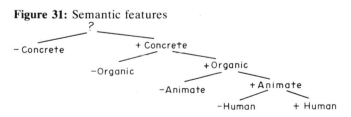

This means that a feature like HUMAN includes all those above it in the hierarchy. To specify a word as having the feature +HUMAN implies that it also has the features +ANIMATE, +ORGANIC and +CONCRETE. But not all features of meaning that can be identified may be hierarchically ordered in this way. To further differentiate the meanings of words with the feature +HUMAN, eg *boy, girl, man, woman*, we need two further features: MALE and ADULT. Not only may these not be hierarchically ordered themselves, since *boy* and *girl* are −ADULT, while *girl* and *woman* are −MALE; but these features are also needed to differentiate words with the feature +ANIMATE which are −HUMAN, eg *mare, stallion, foal*. Incidentally, this set of words also shows that features may be marked ±, since *foal* would be ±MALE.

The implication of distinctive feature analysis, as it is called, is that the whole vocabulary may be differentiated and related by means of features. In this view each lexical item would be decomposed into its distinctive semantic features in the same way that in phonology a phoneme may be decomposed into its distinctive phonetic features, eg /p/ into 'bilabial', 'voiceless' and 'plosive'. However, it is not clear that lexical items and their meanings may be totally analyzed in this way. Take the much analyzed example *bachelor*. In terms of the features so far considered, *bachelor* is presumably + HUMAN, + MALE and + ADULT. We shall now require a further feature MARRIED, which will also be required for the word *spinster*, and both of these will be −MARRIED. This analysis accounts for only one sense of the word *bachelor*, ie that meaning 'an unmarried man'; it does not, for example, account for the sense 'holder of a first degree of a university'.

Our analysis for this one sense is, however, reasonably successful in terms of features: the meaning of *bachelor* is well represented by the features +HUMAN, +MALE, +ADULT, −MARRIED. But take the word *table*. In terms of the features already considered, this is presumably analyzable as +CONCRETE and −ORGANIC. Beyond this, we probably need a feature FURNITURE, and *table* will be marked as +FURNITURE. After this we begin to get stuck. Is the fact that a table has a flat surface and stands on legs of criterial significance? Or should we concentrate on its use? But many items of furniture have flat surfaces and stand on legs—cabinets, desks, cupboards, bookcases. And could we define its use precisely enough?—for eating off? for working at? And would these be universal semantic features?

Some areas of vocabulary do, however, lend themselves well to a feature type of analysis. This is particularly the case with kinship terms. To distinguish the words *mother, father, son, daughter, brother, sister, uncle, aunt, cousin, niece* and *nephew* the following features are needed: MALE, SAME GENERATION, ASCENDING GENERATION, COLLATERAL.

Exercise 32

Work out a matrix to analyze the kinship terms in the previous paragraph, using the features given. Put the kinship terms down the left-hand side of the matrix and the features across the top.

Sense relations

Another way of relating vocabulary items to each other is by means of the so-called

sense relations. Meaning, it is argued, involves on the one hand the relation of reference to extralinguistic reality, and on the other relations of 'sense' to other vocabulary items. Four main sense relations have been identified: synonymy, antonymy, hyponymy and incompatibility.

Synonymy and **antonymy** are concerned with 'sameness' and 'oppositeness' of meaning respectively. So *liberty* and *freedom* are said to be synonyms, while *freedom* and *captivity* could be classed as antonyms.

However, synonymy is a rather slippery notion, since whether two words are considered to be synonyms depends to a large extent on how the notion of synonymy is defined. The most rigid definition would demand the total inter-changeability of words in all contexts of use. This definition would exclude the recognition of *liberty* and *freedom* as synonyms, since one can talk about the *freedom of speech* but not about the *liberty of speech*. In fact, under this kind of definition few words in the language would have synonyms. This is to be expected, since a principle of economy seems to operate in language to ensure that there is not vast redundant choice. If two words with approximately the same meaning occur in a language, there is a tendency to make a differentiation in usage, so that the choice between them becomes meaningful and not redundant.

But synonymy can be defined in a much looser fashion eg as the sameness of core or cognitive meaning. This would exclude emotive meaning, connotations and special usages from the definition. By means of such a definition many words in the vocabulary may be related to each other in terms of synonymy, as Roget's *Thesaurus of English words and phrases* demonstrates. Roget also operates with the notion of antonymy; the parallel columns on the page of the Thesaurus contain lists of synonyms in a relation of antonymy.

It is possible to distinguish two kinds of antonymy. One kind is illustrated by the pair of opposites *tall* and *short*. To say that somebody is *not tall* does not necessarily imply that they are *short*, and to say that somebody is *not short* does not necessarily mean that they are *tall*. These are **gradable** antonyms; we can say of someone: *He is taller than Jim, but shorter than Alfred*. The other kind of antonymy is illustrated by the pair of words *buy* and *sell*. These words are said to be **converses** of each other: if someone buys from someone else it implies that the latter sells to the former. Further examples of converses are: *give* and *receive, husband* and *wife*.

Hyponymy is a paradigmatic relation between words which refers to the inclusion of the meaning of one word in that of another. It implies a superordinate and a subordinate term. For example, the meaning of *scarlet* is included within the meaning of *red*; it is said to be a hyponym of *red*. The meanings of *tulip, daffodil,* and *rose* are included within that of *flower*; they are co-hyponyms of *flower*. The implication of hyponymy is, perhaps, that the vocabulary of a language has a hierarchical organization, with hyponyms of hyponyms of hyponyms as the meaning of the words becomes more general and more inclusive. For example, *dog* is a hyponym of *animal*, which is a hyponym of *mammal*, which is a hyponym of *creature*. But not all the words in the vocabulary of English can be considered to be ordered in this kind of hierarchy. Many words appear to have no superordinate term in which they are included, eg *think, colour*. The relation among co-hyponyms is one of incompatibility, and this relation applies also to sets of words which have no superordinate term. The colour words, for example, are incompatible: to say that something is *red* is to deny that it is *green, blue, yellow* etc. To say that something is a *tree* is to deny that it is a *shrub, bush, plant* etc. Incompatibility is a relation that holds between items which have a similar meaning, or which refer in the same general area of meaning.

Lexical fields

A third attempt to relate vocabulary items in a basically paradigmatic way is by means of the notion of **lexical fields**, which are also sometimes called semantic fields or semantic domains, or lexical sets. A lexical field is a set of lexical items related in meaning and arrayed to display the similarities and differences between the items. In Figure 32 are set out the lexical fields of *cook* and *noise**. The implication of this approach to the study of lexical relations is that the vocabulary of a language can be divided up into a number of lexical fields, exhaustively. It is an approach that is reflected in foreign-language courses that use a 'situational' approach, with lessons entitled 'at the bank', 'at the hotel', 'buying vegetables' etc. In fact, a language cannot be exhaustively divided up in this way, just as a culture does not show clear demarcation lines between all its parts. Linguistically, the presence of a large number of 'core' words that occur in numerous lexical sets or perhaps in the social situations associated with them present problems for this kind of attempt. However, a large number of lexical fields can be identified in a language and they do present us with an interesting insight into the structure of vocabulary. Roget's *Thesaurus* is based in part, at least implicitly, on this kind of approach.

In selecting words for inclusion in a particular lexical field, the principle of loose synonymy is applied: the words selected are related in meaning, not in the sense that they are necessarily interchangeable, but in the sense that they refer to the same area of reality or experience. The relation of hyponymy is also important, since where possible words are arranged hierarchically in a lexical field, with superordinate and subordinate terms; eg *cook* is a superordinate term for most of the terms in that field. In order to distinguish the terms in a lexical field the technique of feature analysis is often used. So, for the cooking terms, features like ±WATER, ±OIL, ±INSIDE OVEN would be necessary to distinguish the terms in that field.

In the lexical field of the verbs of motion features like the following will be needed: LIMBS USED, ORDER OF CONTACT WITH SURFACE, SUBSTANCE (water, air), HORIZONTAL OR VERTICAL MOTION, CONTINUOUS CONTACT etc. These will distinguish items like: *walk, run, crawl, swim, climb, creep, ride, fly, sail, move.*

Note

* Reproduced from Lehrer, A, *Semantic fields and lexical structure* North Holland Publishing Co, 1974. pp. 31 and 40.

Figure 32: Lexical fields of *cook* and *noise*

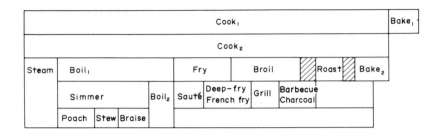

Synonyms appear in the same square. Incompatible terms are separated by vertical lines. Shaded areas indicate overlap. *Grill* is largely subordinate to *broil* (in American English), but there is some overlap with *fry*.

For some speakers, *steam* is included in $boil_1$.

Boil$_1$		
Steam	Simmer	Boil$_2$

Sound = noise$_1$		
(Audible)		(Inaudible)
Loud ⟷	Soft = quiet$_2$	Silent = quiet$_1$
Noise$_2$		Hush$_1$ Mute Still
Din Racket Clamor Shrill Screech Deafening Ear-splitting Crash Clatter Rattle Strident	Resounding Resonant Sonorous Hushed$_2$ Muffled	

Exercise 33

Indicate a hierarchical ordering among the verbs of motion given in the final paragraph above, and attempt to relate them by means of feature analysis, in the following matrix:

	walk	run	crawl	swim	climb	creep	ride	fly	sail	move
FEET										
HANDS										
BODY										
CONTACT										
EARTH										
WATER										
VEHICLE										
VERTICAL										

Conclusion and further reading

We have now looked at each of the three main areas of the linguistic description of English and proposed methods and techniques of analysis for each of them. It must be said, however, that not every possible aspect of English has been dealt with. There is much that in an introductory work of this kind could only be touched on or not considered at all. For example, comparatively little has been said about the whole complex area of tense and aspect in English, and inevitably not every possible kind of clause or sentence structure or kind of word derivation or compounding has received a mention. But the reader who has worked his way through the book should now have enough knowledge and experience to tackle any structure of English he may care to analyze, though probably, in the case of more complex structures, with the help of some of the reference books now available.

We will now consider and recommend some reference books and further reading for each of the three areas of linguistic description, and for linguistics generally.

A very useful coursebook in phonetics, though rather sparse on intonation, is *Practical phonetics* by J C Wells and G Colson, published in 1971 by Pitman. The classic and very detailed description of the phonetics of English is A C Gimson's *An introduction to the pronunciation of English*, published by Edward Arnold in a 3rd edition in 1980. A book devoted entirely to the intonation of English is *Intonation of colloquial English* by J D O'Connor and G F Arnold, published in 1961 by Longman. And finally, for a more wide-ranging introduction to phonetics, look at J D O'Connor's *Phonetics*, published by Penguin in 1973.

The main reference work to be cited in the area of grammar is the one already mentioned a number of times: *A grammar of contemporary English* by R Quirk, S Greenbaum, G Leech and J Svartvik, first published by Longman in 1972. Several smaller—and cheaper—works derived from the *Grammar of contemporary English* have been published subsequently by Longman and the reader may find one of these more suitable to his purposes—and his pocket. R. Quirk and S Greenbaum collaborated on *A university grammar of English*, published in 1973, and G Leech and J Svartvik produced *A communicative grammar of English*, published in 1975, which presents English grammar from the viewpoint of its communicative functions. A third derivative is R A Close's *A reference grammar for students of English*, published in 1975, which is intended mainly for students of English as a foreign language and differs in some respects from the other grammars.

In the field of text grammar, a rather long-winded but quite detailed treatment of cohesion can be found in *Cohesion in English* by M A K Halliday and R Hasan, published in 1976 by Longman. A more general reference work covering in great detail many aspects of text-grammar is *A text grammar of English* by E Werlich, published in Germany in 1976 by Quelle & Meyer.

In the area of words let us recommend first of all two dictionaries: the *Longman Dictionary of contemporary English*, published in 1978, and the *Oxford advanced learner's dictionary of current English*, edited in a 3rd edition by A S Hornby and published by Oxford University Press in 1975. Both are intended primarily for students of English as a foreign language, but they contain the kind of information about words that a serious mother-tongue student of English should expect to find in a dictionary. An interesting book is *Dictionaries and that Dictionary*, edited by J Sledd and W R Ebbitt and published in 1962 by Scott Foresman. It deals in particular with the reception of *Webster's third international dictionary of the English language* (G & C Merriam Co, 1961), the 'that dictionary' of the title.

Mention ought to be made here of an alternative reference work on words, which organizes vocabulary in other than an alphabetical listing: Roget's *Thesauraus of English words and phrases*, which arranges the vocabulary of English according to the principles of synonymy and antonymy in a series of sections and sub-sections containing related words. It was published originally in 1852, then in a new edition by Longman in 1936, and is now available in a number of editions. A more recent attempt to present vocabulary in lexical fields is the *Longman lexicon of contemporary English*, compiled by T McArthur and published in 1981: it is less comprehensive than Roget, but it does provide dictionary-type information for every word.

On the topic of morphology P H Matthews' *Morphology*, published by Cambridge University Press in 1974, is a good and comprehensive account, though in no way restricted to English. And in F R Palmer's *Grammar* (Penguin, 1971) morphology in general is dealt with and some aspects of the morphology of English.

Among other books dealing with words and meanings from various points of view, the following are worth looking at: *Semantic fields and lexical structure* by A Lehrer (North Holland Publishing Co, 1974); *Understanding Language* (Chapters 3 and 4) by R Fowler (Routledge and Kegan Paul, 1974); and *Introduction to theoretical linguistics* (Chapters 9 and 10) by J Lyons (Cambridge University Press, 1968).

For readers wishing to investigate the wider issues of descriptive and theoretical linguistics, D Bolinger's *Aspects of Language* is a good book to start with. It was published by Harcourt Brace Jovanovich in a 3rd edition in 1981 and is a readable and wide-ranging account of many of the topics of concern to scholars in all branches of linguistics. Less wide-ranging but quite broad in its coverage is J Lyons' *Language and Linguistics*, published by Longman in 1981. These could be followed up by R H Robins' *General linguistics, An introductory survey* (3rd edition, Longman, 1980), or R Fowler's *Understanding Language* (RKP, 1974), or D J Allerton's *Essentials of grammatical theory* (RKP, 1979), or P H Matthews' *Syntax* (Cambridge University Press, 1981).

Those interested in following up particular schools of linguistics, or particular issues in linguistics, or in the description of English will find further references in the bibliographies of the books mentioned in this conclusion.

Key to exercises

Exercise 1

1. voiceless alveolar plosive
2. voiced labio-dental fricative
3. voiceless velar plosive
4. voiceless dental fricative
5. voiced alveolar nasal
6. open back spread vowel (for southerners), open front spread vowel (for Midlanders and Northerners)
7. voiceless bilabial plosive
8. close front spread vowel
9. open back rounded vowel
10. voiced alveolar lateral
11. voiced velar plosive
12. voiced alveolar fricative

Exercise 2

1. ʃɛd
2. tiθ
3. tʃɑt
4. dɪtɛst
5. dʒɛt
6. gɑd
7. ðiz
8. bɑdʒ
9. vɑz
10. ʃɛf
11. pitʃ
12. θiv
13. jist
14. grin
15. mɑz
16. wɛlθ
17. hil
18. rɛntʃ
19. kris
20. tʃɑdʒ
21. ʃrik
22. flɪŋ
23. stɪŋk
24. jild

Exercise 3

1. /kɔt/
2. /ənʌðə/
3. /feɪnt/
4. /sɒk/
5. /bæg/
6. /kʌvə/
7. /tɜn/
8. /fjʊəl/
9. /kaʊnt/
10. /lʊk/
11. kætʃɪŋ/
12. /taɪl/
13. /lɑdʒ/
14. /bɛg/
15. /dʌzən/
16. /dɜtɪ/
17. /ʃɛə/
18. /gəʊl/
19. /fud/
20. /flɛʃ/
21. /fɪə/
22. /fɔl/
23. /mɒnɪŋ/
24. /plizd/
25. /kənfɛs/
26. /mɒɪst/
27. /pleɪn/
28. /sɒlt/ or /sɔlt/
29. /lɜkɪŋ/
30. /klaɪm/

Exercise 4

1. /pleɪgraʊnd/
2. /flɛksɪbəl/
3. /tʃaɪniz/
4. /drʌdʒərɪ/
5. /ɪnsɪnjueɪʃən/
6. /plɛʒərəbəl/
7. /blɪŋkəz/
8. /ʌndəsteɪt/
9. /sɜtʃwɔrənt/
10. /blækmeɪl/
11. /maɪgreɪʃən/
12. /frikwənsɪ/
13. /rəʊbʌst/
14. /fɔsɛps/
15. /pærənɒɪə/
16. /bɜθdeɪ/
17. /keədfɔ/
18. raɪðɪŋ/
19. /kjʊə(r)əl/
20. /əʊvəɛstɪmeɪt/

Exercise 5

1. /frik/ [f̥ɹikʰ]
2. /wɛlθ/ [w̥ɛɫθ]
3. /kɛtəl/ [kʰɛtʰəɬ]
4. /plɪnθ/ [pʰlɪnθ]
5. /θɜzdɪ/ [θɜːzdɪ]
6. /ətʃiv/ [ətʃiːɣ] or [ətʃiːv]
7. /gɔdʒəs/ [g̃ɔːdʒəs]

138

8. /kʌmfətəbəl/   [kʰʌɱf(ə)tʰəbəɫ] or [kʰʌmf(ə)tʰəbəɫ]
9. /pɜkʌʃən/   [pʰɜkʰʌʃən]
10. /raɪð/   [ɹaɪːð̩] or [ɫaɪːð]
11. /ælkəhɒl/   [ætkʰəhɒɫ]
12. /θɜstɪ/   [θɜstɪ]
13. /rɪdʒɛkt/   [ɹɪdʒɛkʰtʰ]
14. /prəʊb/   [pʰɹ̥əʊːb̩] or [pʰɹ̥əʊːb]
15. /ɪspɛʃəlɪ/   [ɪspɛʃ(ə)lɪ]
16. /maɪld/   [maɪːɫd̩] or [maɪːɫd]
17. /kɔstɪk/   [kʰɔstɪkʰ]
18. /pærəmaʊnt/   [pʰærəmaʊːntʰ] or [pʰæləmaʊːnʔ]
19. /kənvɜʃən/   [kʰəɱvɜʃən] or [kʰənvɜʃən]
20. /plizɪŋ/   [pʰɹ̥iːzɪŋ]
21. /feɪvərɪt/   [feɪːvərɪtʰ] or [feɪːvəɹɪʔ]
22. /rɪsiv/   [ɹɪsiːv̥] or [ɹɪsiːv]
23. /ʌnʃɔ/   [ʌnʃɔː]
24. /əbleɪz/   [əbleɪːz̥] or [əbleɪːz]
25. /skritʃ/   [skɹ̥itʃ]

Exercise 6

1. [ðeɪ tʰɹ̥eɪːŋ kʰaʊs tʰʊ dʒʌmpʰ]
2. [ə bæb pʰɪkʰtʃə əv ə ɹəʊs tʰɹ̥iː]
3. [huː dʒuː wɒntʰ]
4. [hɪ wəʃ ʃɪpʰɹ̥ɛ kʰtʰ]
5. [hɪs faʊnt sɛvəɱ feɪp pʰɪkʰtʃəz]

Exercise 7

1. [wɒ dɪdʒuː seɪ ɪz neɪːm wəz]
2. [wɪ dɪskʌs ðɪ aɪːdɪə ɫ əv aɪːvənz lɑs tʃuːzdɪ]
3. [ɪ dɪgŋ kʰʌm tʰə ðə lɛkʰtʃə ɫ ɔː ɪ wʊd əv nəʊːn]
4. [ðeɪ kˈʰæmp baɪː ðə ɹɪvə ɫ ɒn ðɪ ʌðə saɪːd̩]
5. [ðə mɑsk gʌmmən ɛɫd ðɪ ɒstɪdʒ ək gʌmpʰɒɪː ntʰ]

Exercise 8

One example only for each of the combinations is given.

/sm/	smell	/sn/	sniff	/st/	stuck	/sk/	skip
/sp/	spell	/sf/	sphere	/dw/	dwell	/θw/	thwart
/tw/	twenty	/dr/	drive	/θr/	thread	/tr/	tree
/kw/	queen	/kr/	cream	/kl/	clod	/pr/	prune
/fr/	friend	/br/	break	/gr/	grave	/pl/	play
/fl/	float	/bl/	blade	/gl/	glad	/ʃr/	shred
/sw/	swim	/sl/	sleep				
/spl/	splice	/spr/	spray	/sfr/	sphragistics		
/str/	straight	/skr/	scrape	/skw/	squeal		

Exercise 9

1. maˈchine
2. ˈfeˌmale
3. ˌmaˈgazine
4. ˈquan ti ty
5. ˈte leˌphone
6. ˌrhiˈno ce ros
7. ˈco ward li ness
8. ˌsa tisˈfac to ry
9. inˌfe riˈo ri ty
10. perˌso ni fiˈca tion
11. ˌu niˈla te ra lism

Exercise 10

1. ˇTHAT
2. ˋYESterday
3. ˊTHAT
4. ˆriDIculous
5. ˋCANT
6. ˋalRIGHT
7. ˌTALKED
8. ˇME or ˇTHERE
9. ˌunderSTAND
10. ˆNEVer

Exercise 11

1.

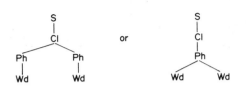

2.

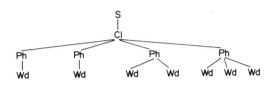

3.

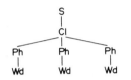

4.

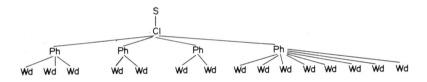

5.

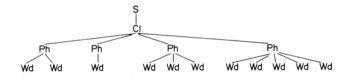

6.

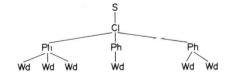

7.

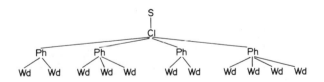

8.

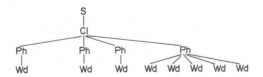

9.

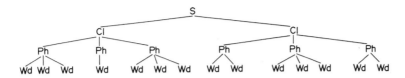

10.

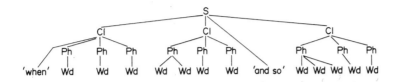

Exercise 12

1. When (conj) April (N) with (prep) his (det) sweet (adj) showers (N) has (V) pierced (V) the (det) drought (N) of (prep) March (N) to (prep) the (det) root (N), then (adv) people (N) wish (V) to go (V) on (prep) pilgrimages (N).
2. Hardly (adv) knowing (V) what (pron) she (pron) did (V), she (pron) picked up (V) a (det) little (adj) (quant) bit (N) of (prep) (or: a little bit of (quant)) stick (N), and (conj) held (V) it (pron) out (adv) to (prep) the (det) puppy (N).
3. Alice (N) looked (V) at (prep) the (det) jury-box (N), and (conj) saw (V) that (conj), in (prep) her (det) haste (N), she (pron) had (V) put (V) the (det) Lizard (N) in (adv) head (N) downwards (adv), and (conj) the (det) poor (adj) little (adj) thing (N) was (V) waving (V) its (det) tail (N) about (adv) in (prep) a (det) melancholy (adj) way (N), being (V) quite (adv) unable (adj) to move (V).
4. To gain (V) the (det) maximum (adj) amount (N) of (prep) fruit (N) from (prep) a (det) strawberry (N) bed (N) a (det) certain (adj) amount (N) of (prep) attention (N) is (V) needed (V) now (adv).
5. By (prep) this (det) time (N) of (prep) year (N) most (pron) of (prep) us (pron) are (V) viewing (V) our (det) flower (N) borders (N) with (prep) a (det) fairly (adv) critical (adj) eye (N), noting (V) spaces (N) where (pron) improvements (N) can (V) be (V) made (V).

Exercise 13

1. five (num) green (adj) bottles (head)
2. my (ident) third (num) currant (N mod) bun (head)
3. Jim's (NP gen) many (quant) fatal (adj) mistakes (head)
4. all (pre-det) our (ident) many (quant) grievous (adj) sins (head)
5. an (ident) ugly (adj) large (adj) yellow (adj) submarine (head)
6. plenty of (quant) delicious (adj) rice (N mod) pudding (head)
7. this mischievous tax collector's (NP gen) grabbing (adj) hand (head); this (ident)mischievous (adj) tax (N mod) collector (head)
8. his (ident) underrated (adj) musical (adj) talent (head)
9. her (ident) blue (adj) collapsible (adj) silk (N mod) umbrella (head)
10. all our relations' (NP gen) dirty (adj) screaming (adj) offspring (head); all (pre Det) our (ident) relations (head).

Exercise 14

1. the (ident) old (adj) cupboard (head) with the blue handles (post mod prep P)
2. all (pre-det) the (ident) coal (head) stacked outside the back door (post mod non-finite cl)
3. the (ident) third (num) unpleasant (adj) task (head) to be assigned to me (post mod non-fin cl)

4. the (ident) fourth (num) place (head) behind Jim (post mod prep P)
5. the (ident) major (adj) upset (head) of the year (post mod prep P)
6. the (ident) clearest (adj) instructions (head) that anybody could have been given (post mod rel cl)
7. this (ident) sudden (adj) disaster (head) approaching us (post mod non-fin cl)
8. all (pre-det) the (ident) eighty (num) elderly (adj) passengers (head) in the first coach (post mod prep P)
9. several (quant) irate (adj) gentleman (N mod) farmers (head) waiting for the Prime Minister (post mod non-fin cl)
10. a (ident) poor (adj) little (adj) boy (head) who seems to be lost (post mod rel cl)

Exercise 15

1. may (modal) have (perfective) sat (lexical past part)
2. can (modal) not (neg) have (perf) been (progressive) singing (lexical pres part)
3. have (perf) been (prog) drinking (lexical pres part)
4. are (prog) being (passive) stopped (lexical past part)
5. does ('do') not (neg) know (lexical infinitive)
6. would (modal) not (neg) have (perf) been (passive) caught (lexical past part)
7. can (modal) not (neg) have (perf) been (prog) being (pass) executed (lexical past part)
8. have (perf) not (neg) finished (lexical past part)
9. might (modal) be (pass) seen (lexical past part)
10. has (perf) been (prog) being (pass) heated (lexical past part).

Exercise 16

1. NP; a (ident) very earnest (adj P) look (head); very (intens adv) earnest (head adj)
2. he (NP) sounds (VP) very interested in our proposal (adj P); he (head N) sounds (lex V) very (intens adv) interested (head adj) in our proposal (comp prep P); in (prep) our proposal (NP); our (ident) proposal (head N)
3. unfortunately (adv P disj) he (NP) is (VP) very busy (adj P) now (adv P adju); very (intens adv) busy (head adj)
4. NP; a (ident) quite ridiculously worded (adjP) statement (head N); quite ridiculously (adv P) worded (head adj); quite (intens adv) ridiculously (head adv)
5. is (VP) he (NP) certain of our support (adj P); certain (head adj) of our support (comp prep P); of (prep) our support (NP); our (ident) support (head N)
6. I (NP) am (VP) quite sure that he is certain to win (adj P); quite (intens adv) sure (head adj) that he is certain to win (comp that-cl); that (conj) he (NP) is (VP) certain to win (adj P); certain (head adj) to win (comp inf-cl)
7. NP; a (ident) rather baffling (adj P) description (head N); rather (intens adv) baffling (head adj)
8. so (adv conju) that (NP) makes (VP) it (NP) awkward to find (adj P); awkward (head adj) to find (comp inf-cl)
9. astonishingly (adv disj) he (NP) can walk (VP) very fast (adv P); can (modal) walk (lex V); very (intens adv) fast (head adv)
10. he (NP) was (VP) rather concerned that no one should know immediately (adj P); rather (intens adv) concerned (head adj) that no one should know immediately (comp that-cl); that (conj) no one (NP) should know (VP) immediately (adv P); should (modal) know (lex V).

Exercise 17

1. The farmer (S:NP) was eating (V:VP) his lunch (O:NP) in the corn field (A:prep P).
2. The committee (S:NP) considers (V:VP) your proposals (O:NP) rather unworkable (C:adj P).
3. The transport manager (S:NP) could not decide on (V:VP) a new bus (O:NP)—or: could not decide (V:VP) on a new bus (O:prep P).
4. Jim (S:NP) passed (V:VP) the salt (O:NP) down the table (A:prep P).

5. The delinquent (S:NP) received (V:VP) a reprimand (O:NP) from the magistrate (O:prep P).
6. The milk (S:NP) has gone (V:VP) sour (C:adj P).
7. Gordon (S:NP) sent (V:VP) his apologies (O:NP) to the meeting (O or A:prep P).

Exercise 18

1. The old fellow (S:NP) forgot about (V:VP) Jim (O:NP) yesterday (A:NP). Type 4.
2. I (S:NP) wouldn't make (V:VP) rice (O:NP) in that saucepan (A:prep P). Type 4.
3. Your Madras curry (S:NP) smells (V:VP) appetizing (C:adj P). Type 3.
4. You (S:NP) may not deposit (V:VP) your boots (O:NP) on top of mine (A:prep P). Type 5.
5. They (S:NP) rolled (V:VP) the barrel (O:NP) into the courtyard (A:prep P). Type 4.
6. You (S:NP) must not walk (V:VP) on the grass (A:prep P). Type 2.
7. They (S:NP) consider (V:VP) poor old Andrei (O:NP) insane (C:adj P). Type 7.
8. Barry (S:NP) sent (V:VP) Mary (Oi:NP) a bunch of carnations (Od:NP). Type 6.
9. Your luggage (S:NP) weighs (V:VP) seventy kilos (A:NP). Type 2.
10. The children (S:NP) played (V:VP) in the garden (A:prep P) all yesterday afternoon (A:NP). Type 1.

Exercise 19

1. That people throw away money on gambling (S:that-cl) never (A:adv P) ceases (V:VP) to amaze me (O:inf cl).
2. I (S:NP) cannot imagine (V:VP) how the mistake could have happened (O:wh-cl).
3. He (S:NP) doesn't seem (V:VP) to suffer much (C:inf cl).
4. You (S:NP) cannot order (V:VP) me (Oi:NP) to jump into the river (O:inf cl).
5. I (S:NP) think (V:VP) that you will catch him stealing the apples (O:that-cl).
6. They (S:NP) reported (V:VP) to the police (Oi:prep P) what the prisoner had said (Od:wh-cl).
7. It (dummy) disappointed (V:VP) the candidate (O:NP) that few people came to hear him (S:that-cl).
8. We (S:NP) do not know (V:VP) who will be his successor (O:wh-cl).

Exercise 20

1.

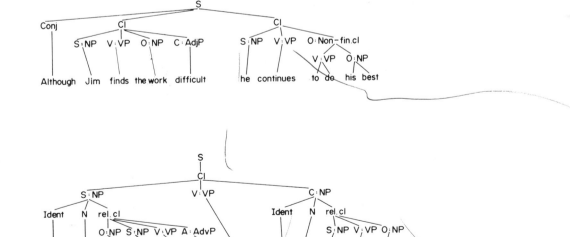

2.

3.

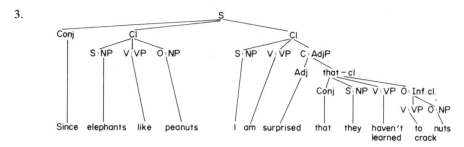

4.

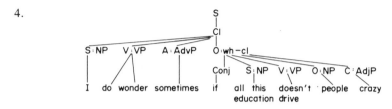

5.

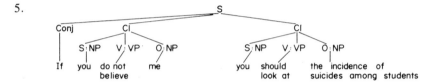

6.

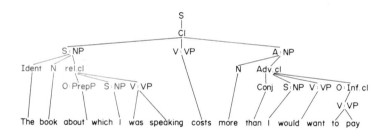

7.

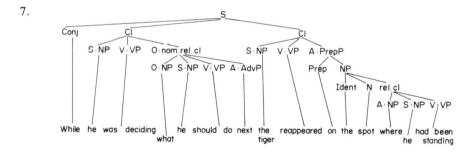

8.

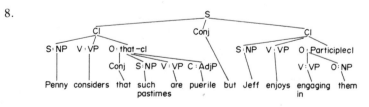

Exercise 21

1.

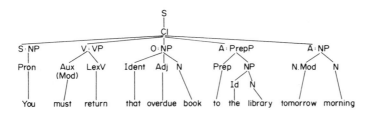

2.

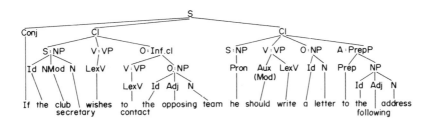

3.

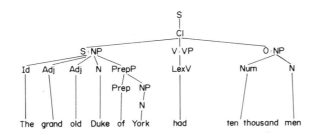

4.

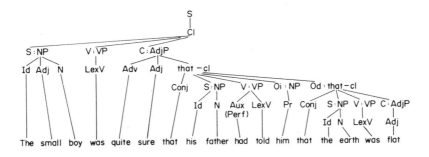

5.

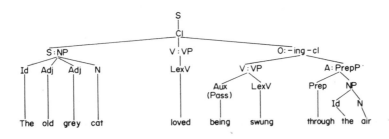

6.

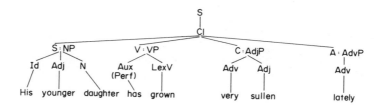

7.

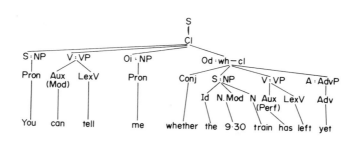

8.

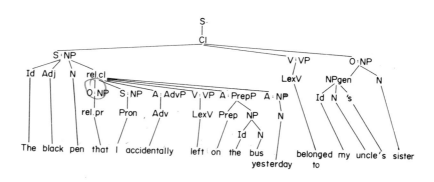

9.

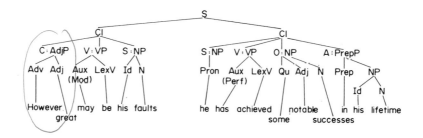

10.

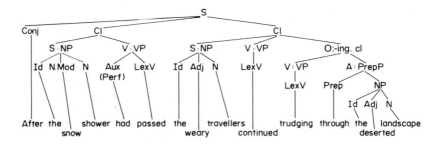

11.

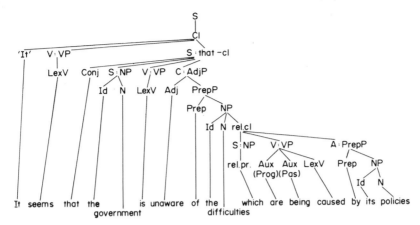

12.

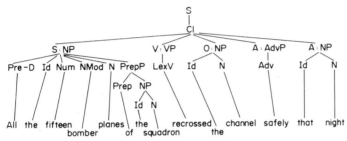

Exercise 22

1. eg For his first birthday the old man sent his . . .
   To his favourite grandson the old man sent . . .
   It was a wooden lorry that the old man sent . . ., etc.
2. eg That Jim would do such a thing I can't believe;
   What I can't do is believe that Jim . . .
3. eg They found guilty the man who had a scar on his cheek;
   They found the man guilty who had a scar . . .
   It was the man who had a scar on his cheek that . . ., etc.
4. eg In the clearing hundreds of elephants were gathering;
   It was in the clearing that hundreds of elephants . . .
   What the hundreds of elephants were doing was gathering . . ., etc.
5. eg It is no easy task for a woman to change a car wheel;
   For a woman it is no easy task to change . . .
   What is no easy task for a woman is changing . . ., etc.

Exercise 23

'It was dreadfully cold, snowing, and turning dark. It was *the* last evening of the year, New Year's Eve. In *this* cold and darkness walked a little girl. *She* was poor and both *her* head and feet were bare. Oh, *she* had had a pair of slippers when *she* left home; *but they* had been too big for *her*—in truth, *they* had belonged to *her* mother. *The* little *one* had lost *them* while hurrying across *the* street to get out of the way of two carriages that had been driving along awfully fast. *One of the* slippers *she* could not find, and *the other* had been snatched by a boy who, laughingly, shouted that *he* would use *it* as a cradle when *he* had a child of *his* own.
'Now *the* little girl walked barefoot through *the* streets. *Her* feet were swollen and red from *the* cold. *She* was carrying a little bundle of matches in *her* hand *and* had *more* in *her* apron pocket. No one had bought *any* all day, *or* given *her* so much as a penny. Cold and hungry, *she* walked through *the* city; cowed by life *the* poor thing!

'*The* snowflakes fell on *her* long yellow hair that curled so prettily at *the* neck, *but* to *such* things *she* never gave a thought. From every window of every house, light shone, *and one* could smell *the* geese roasting all the way out in *the* street. It was, *after all*, New Year's Eve; *and this she* did think about'

Exercise 24

evening: lexical cohesion (collocation) with *dark*.
this cold and darkness: reference + lexical cohesion (reiteration).
she, her: reference.
Oh: ?conjunction.
she: reference.
slippers: lexical cohesion (collocation) with *feet*.
she: reference.
but they: conjunction + reference.
her: reference.
in truth they: conjunction + reference.
her: reference.
the little one: reference + lexical cohesion (reiteration) + substitution.
them: reference.
one of the slippers: reference + lexical cohesion (reiteration).
she: reference.
the other . . .: reference + ellipsis.
he, it, he, his: reference.

Exercise 25

1. *un*—not; *decide; d*—past tense/past participle.
2. *devol(ve); tion*—change verb to noun.
3. *fat(e); al*—change noun to adjective; *ity*——change adjective to noun.
4. *im*—not; *penetra(te); abl(e)*—verb to adjective; *ity*—adjective to noun.
5. *re*—again; *introduc(e); tion*—verb to noun.
6. *make; s*—3rd person singular present tense.
7. *un*—not; *interest; ing*—present participle/noun to adjective.
8. *revenge; ful*—noun to adjective.
9. *wall; flower; s*—plural.
10. *dis*—not; *establish; ed*—past tense/past participle.

Exercise 26

1. *pre-* (D) *determine -d* (I)
2. *re-* (D) *interpret -ing* (I)
3. *ir-* (D) *resist -ible* (D)
4. *?in-* (D) *flam(e) -ation* (D) *-s* (I)
5. *confid(e) -ent* (D) *-ial* (D)
6. *logan-* (?D) *berri -es* (I)
7. *un-* (D) *verbal -ize* (D) *-d* (I)
8. *deaf -en* (D) *-ed* (I)
9. *hope -ful* (D) *-ly* (D)
10. *ironmonger -y* (D)

Exercise 27

1. suffix /-z/
2. suffix /-s/
3. suffix /-ɪz/
4. 'zero' /Ø/
5. vowel change /ʊ/ to /i/
6. vowel change /æ/ to /ɛ/
7. vowel change /aɪ/ to /ɪ/
   and suffix /-lən/

8. vowel change /u/ to /i/
9. suffix /-ən/
10. suffix /-z/ and voicing of final consonant of root.
11. suffix /-z/ and voicing of final consonant of root.

Exercise 28

Past tense	Past participle
1. suffix /-d/	suffix /-d/
2. suffix /-t/	suffix /-t/
3. suffix /-ɪd/	suffix /-ɪd/
4. suffix /Ø/	suffix /Ø/
5. vowel change /ɪ/ to /ʌ/	vowel change /ɪ/ to /ʌ/
6. vowel change /aɪ/ to /aʊ/	vowel change /aɪ/ to /aʊ/
7. vowel change /ɛə/ to /ɔə/	suffix /-n/ and vowel change /ɛə/ to /ɔə/
8. vowel change /ɪ/ to /æ/	vowel change /ɪ/ to /ʌ/
9. vowel change /ʌ/ to /æ/	suffix /Ø/
10. root-final consonant change /d/ to /t/	root-final consonant change /d/ to /t/
11. vowel change /æ/ to /ɔ/ and final consonant /tʃ/ to /t/	vowel change /æ/ to /ɔ/ and final consonant /tʃ/ to /t/
12. vowel change /ɛ/ to /əʊ/ and suffix /-d/	vowel change /ɛ/ to /əʊ/ and suffix /-d/
13. vowel change /i/ to /ɛ/, final consonant devoiced, suffix /-t/	vowel change /i/ to /ɛ/, final consonant devoiced, suffix /-t/
14. suffix /-d/	suffix/-n/
15. vowel change /u/ to /ɪ/, suffix /-d/	vowel change /u/ to /ʌ/, suffix /-n/
16. complete change (suppletion)	vowel change /əʊ/ to /ɒ/, suffix /-n/.

Exercise 29

1. the break *of* day; 2. a bite *from* frost; 3. wood *that* drifts; 4. corn *that has* popped; 5. a shake *by* the hand; 6. 'figuratively', a washing *of* the brain; 7. *one who* makes matches; 8. meat *that has been* minced; 9. water *for* drinking; 10. paper *for* typing *on;* 11. walking *in one's* sleep; 12. *one who* bathes *in* the sun; 13. work *done at* home; 14. bench *for* working *at*; 15. cycle *powered by* a motor; 16. worm *that produces* silk; 17. dust *produced by* sawing; 18. knob *on* a door; 19. tape *used for* measuring; 20. man *who is* 'handy'; 21. drum *shaped like* a kettle; 22. flake *of* soap; 23. shed *for* cows; 24. 'figuratively', like someone with butter on their fingers; 25. 'figuratively', like someone with a high brow.

Exercise 30

bake /beɪk/ v
(1) S V; S V O 'to (cause to) cook using dry heat in an oven'—*to bake bread, the bread is baking*
(2) S V; S V O 'to (cause to) become hard by heating'—*In former times, bricks were baked in the sun until they became hard*
(3) S V infml 'to become hot'—*Open a window, I'm baking in here!*
baker /'beɪkə/ n 'person who bakes bread and cakes, esp. professionally'
bakery /'beɪ kə ri/ n 'a place where bread and sometimes cakes are baked and/or sold'
mislead /mɪs'liːd/ v past tense/past part **misled** /mɪs'lɛd/
S V O:NP (O: *into*—NP, *-ing* -cl) 'to cause (someone) to think or act wrongly or mistakenly; guide wrongly, sometimes with the intention to deceive'—*Her appearance misled him; he thought she was young but she wasn't, Don't let his friendly words mislead you into trusting him*
misleadingly /mɪs'liːd ɪŋ li/ adv.

Exercise 31

1. Subject animate, usually human; object animate, action, quality.
2. Subject animal, *viz* dog, sea-lion, lion, etc; adjunct softly-loudly.
3. Subject animate, usually human; adjunct loudly.
4. Subject human, fact; object assertion, theorem, hypothesis, etc.
5. Subject animal, usually horse, also human; adjunct slowly-fast.
6. Subject human, vessel; object vessel.
7. Subject animate, action; object animate, plan, precious thing.
8. Subject human; adjunct softly-loudly, controllably-uncontrollably.

Exercise 32

	MALE	SAME GEN	ASCENDING GEN	COLLATERAL
father	+	−	+	−
mother	−	−	+	−
son	+	−	−	−
daughter	−	−	−	−
brother	+	+	−	−
sister	−	+	−	−
uncle	+	−	+	+
aunt	−	−	+	+
cousin	±	+	−	+
nephew	+	−	−	+
niece	−	−	−	+

Exercise 33

	walk	run	crawl	swim	climb	creep	ride	fly	sail	move
FEET	+	+	+	+	+	+	−	−	−	±
HANDS	−	−	+	+	+	+	−	−	−	±
BODY	−	−	−	+	−	+	−	−	−	±
CONTACT	+	±	+	+	+	+	−	−	− .	±
EARTH	+	+	+	−	+	+	±	−	−	±
WATER	−	−	−	+	−	−	±	−	+	±
VEHICLE	−	−	−	−	−	−	+	+	+	±
VERTICAL	−	−	−	−	+	−	±	±	−	±

International Phonetic Alphabet

Consonants	Bilabial	Labiodental	Dental and Alveolar	Retroflex	Palato-alveolar	Alveolo-palatal	Palatal	Velar	Uvular	Pharyngal	Glottal
Plosive	p b		t d	ʈ ɖ			c ɟ	k g	q G		ʔ
Nasal	m	ɱ	n	ɳ			ɲ	ŋ	N		
Lateral			l	ɭ			ʎ				
Lateral fricative			ɬ ɮ								
Rolled			r						R		
Flapped			ɾ	ɽ					R		
Rolled fricative			r·								
Fricative	ɸ β	f v	θ ð s z ɹ	ʂ ʐ	ʃ ʒ	ɕ ʑ	ç j	x ɣ	χ ʁ	ħ ʕ	h ɦ
Frictionless Continuants and Semi-vowels	w ɥ	ʋ	ɹ				j (ɥ)	(w) ɣ	ʁ		

Vowels	Rounded			Front Centre Back		
Close	(y ʉ u)			i y · ɨ ʉ · ɯ u		
Half-close	(ø o)			e ø · · ɤ o		
Half-open	(œ ɔ)			ɛ œ · ə · ʌ ɔ		
				· · ɐ ·		
				æ		
Open	(ɒ)			a · ɑ ɒ		

Index